Growing in Christ Together

A 16-Week Discipleship Journey

Justin Kuravackal, Abe Meysenburg,
Jeff Vanderstelt, Brad Watson

Leader Guide

Every Church. Every Person. Every Place

ISBN:
Growing in Christ Together, Leader Guide Paperback: 978-0-9968493-8-8
Growing in Christ Together, Leader Guide ebook: 978-0-9968493-9-5

Cover and book design | Nathan Parry
Editing | Caitlin Wilson

Saturate
227 Bellevue Way NE, #224 Bellevue, WA 98004
www.saturatetheworld.com

Acknowledgements

We owe a tremendous amount to Tim Chester, our brother across the pond in Sheffield, England. He introduced Saturate to several concepts that rapidly became part of the fabric of how we understand and speak about the gospel as a family. For many of us, Tim's ideas have become inextricably woven into what we teach others to help them become more like Jesus and how we live out the gospel in the everyday. Tim later published these thoughts in You Can Change - apart from the Bible, the best book we have read on the gospel and becoming more like Jesus. We've used endnotes with page references to credit him. We highly recommend purchasing the book to dive deeper into discipleship in community.

Table of Contents

INTRODUCTION TO

DNA GROUPS

The term "DNA group" refers to a group that ideally consists of three people—men with men, women with women—who meet together weekly. DNA groups provide a structure for us to care deeply for one another and to foster growth as disciples of Jesus. (For more on the structure and number of participants of a DNA Group, see Appendix 1.)

DNA is an acronym that reminds of us three key components of discipleship: discover, nurture, and act. The goal is to help one another discover Jesus in the Scriptures, nurture the truths of the gospel in our hearts, and faithfully act on what the Spirit calls us to do.

Video: "The Role of DNA Groups"—Abe Meysenburg teaches on what DNA groups are and why they're important. https://saturatetheworld.com/dna-resources/

Our DNA group should be a major factor in our growth as a disciple, someone who is learning to apply the gospel to absolutely every part of life.

Why Should I Be in a DNA Group?

As disciples who've been saved and made righteous, Paul exhorts us to "be transformed by the renewing of your minds" (Romans 12:2). Discipleship requires life-on-life interaction and can only happen in community. We grow primarily through the experience of life in gospel community. A DNA group can be a key catalyst for growth and transformation in our lives.

One of the main ways this happens is by giving each other regular reminders of the truth of the gospel. Hebrews 3:12 (ESV) warns, "Take care, brothers and sisters, lest there be in any of you an evil, unbelieving heart, leading you to fall away from the living God." We are often tempted to forget who God is, what He's done for us in Christ Jesus, who we are as a result, and how we live out of our new identity. Hebrews 3:13 (ESV) says one of the major ways to prevent this "falling away from the living God" is to "encourage one another daily . . . so that none of you may be hardened by the deceitfulness of sin."

Every single day we need to be encouraged with the truth that we are deeply loved and accepted by the Father purely on the basis of what Jesus has done! Our new identity as sons and daughters of God shapes everything about our life as disciples of Jesus. Understanding this new identity also gives us the boldness and humility to be honest with our DNA partners when we are tempted to hide our sin or to blame others. Regular encouragement from our DNA partners can be a significant help in our battle against sin and against the lies of the enemy.

What is the Goal of DNA Groups?

The overall goal of a DNA group is to foster discipleship relationships that help each person grow to become more like Jesus by the power of the Holy Spirit. The goal is not merely to hang out and have fun, or even to build friendships, though hopefully all of that will happen! The goal is to challenge one another to "grow in the grace and knowledge of our Lord and Savior Jesus Christ" (2 Peter 3:18).

As disciples, we should experience transformation at every level, affecting our whole person: head, heart, and hands. The specific discipleship goals for a DNA group meeting can be understood by unpacking the acronym:

Discover: Led by the Holy Spirit, the group will study the Bible and ask the Four Questions. The goal is to teach the head.

Nurture: Led by the Holy Spirit, the group will repent and believe in the gospel. The goal is to shepherd the heart.

Act: Led by the Holy Spirit, the group will listen and obey as He calls us to bear fruit in keeping with repentance. The goal is to empower the hands.

The "Discover-Nurture-Act" Process

At each meeting, a DNA group should walk through the three-step process of discover, nurture, and act. Each of these can only be done with the help of the Holy Spirit, so praying throughout the process is imperative.

Video: "Details of a DNA"—Jeff Vanderstelt teaches on what DNA groups are, why we do them, tips, and the process of discover, nurture, and act. https://saturatetheworld.com/dna-resources/

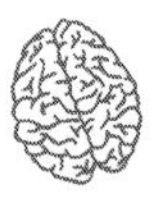

Discover

Led by the Holy Spirit, the group will study the Bible and ask the Four Questions: Who is God, What has He done, Who are we, and How do we live? The goal is to teach the head so each person either learns or is reminded of the truth about who God is, what He's done, who we are, and how we live, every time the DNA group meets.

Discover primarily involves discipling the head. In John 8:31–32 (NIV), Jesus said, "If you hold to my teaching, you are really my disciples. Then you will know the truth, and the truth will set you free." Discover is about uncovering the vital truth about who God is, what He's done, who we are, and how we should live.

A number of Jesus' statements from John's gospel highlights the importance of His word and His Spirit in helping a disciple discover truth:

Jesus prayed, "Sanctify them by the truth; your word is truth." —John 17:17

But the Helper, the Holy Spirit, whom the Father will send in my name, he will teach you all things and bring to your remembrance all that I have said to you. —John 14:26 (ESV)

When the Spirit of truth comes, he will guide you into all the truth, for he will not speak on his own authority, but whatever he hears he will speak, and he will declare to you the things that are to come. He will glorify me, for he will take what is mine and declare it to you. —John 16:13–14 (ESV)

Jesus' death on the cross makes it possible for the Holy Spirit to live in us! His Spirit is our teacher, the one who makes Jesus even more real to us as we grow in our faith. Our motivation to discover comes from the great gift Jesus has given us and from our desire to know Him more. Discover is not about information but about relationship and transformation.

In light of Jesus' prayer in John 17:17, studying the Bible should be the primary way DNA groups discover together. As a group, choose a passage of scripture and read it throughout the week. Each person should utilize the Four Questions as he or she studies on his or her own. Consider using a journal to capture key thoughts and insights that the Spirit brings to mind. Group members should come to the weekly meeting ready to answer these three questions:

1. What did you discover this week? What did you learn? What were you reminded of?
2. Where did the Spirit lead you to repentance and faith this week?
3. How have you struggled with sin/unbelief in your life this week?

When the group meets, pray and ask the Holy Spirit to speak through His word! Read through the whole passage once or twice together. Share any insights from the week, and write down new things the Spirit illuminates.

Discover in This Guide

This book will guide your group toward the regular rhythm of discovering the word of God together and apart. We've set up each week to have specific Scriptures to read, articles to dive into, and questions to process that will lay the foundation for future DNA discussions long after you've put this guide away.

Nurture

Led by the Holy Spirit, the group will repent and believe in the gospel. The goal is to shepherd the heart so each person is brought to repentance and renewed faith every time a DNA group meets.

Nurture primarily involves discipling the heart. The word heart is used more than 850 times in the Bible and is used to describe the very center of our being. It includes our mind, our emotions, and our will. In Romans 10:10 (AMP), Paul says it's the part of us that exercises faith or belief. "For with the heart a person believes. . . ."

In Luke 6, Jesus says the fruit of a person's life—their words and their actions—is an indicator of what is present in his or her heart. "Each tree is known by its own fruit . . . out of the abundance of the heart his mouth speaks" (Luke 6:44–45 ESV). So regardless of what we know in our heads, the fruit of our lives is determined by what we believe in our hearts. We may know God is great and in control and affirm His sovereignty and power, yet we worry. What we know does not align with what we believe in that moment.

When we worry, we're placing our hope in something other than God. We're believing that something other than Him is in control and can give us security. Paul's assessment of this misplaced belief is that we've ". . . exchanged the truth about God for a lie and worshiped and served the creature rather than the Creator" (Romans 1:25 ESV). By placing our faith in something other than God to give us what only He can give, we are actually engaging in false worship, in idolatry.

DNA groups are designed to help identify these areas of sin and idolatry in our lives. Nurture is about ensuring what we know aligns with what we believe.

It is possible to be overzealous in our desire to root sin out of one another's lives. Nurture is not a witch-hunt or a game of "whack-a-mole," where we wait anxiously with a big mallet, smacking down every little indicator of sin and unbelief as it pops up in people's lives.

In reality, we should be even more quick to point out evidences of grace than we are to call out sin or to start poking around, looking for evidence of unbelief.

However, the fundamental assumption is that within a week's time every believer is going to sin and therefore needs to:

- Confess our sins to one another (James 5:16)
- Repent before God (Revelation 3:19)
- Turn back toward Jesus in faith (Hebrews 12:1–2)
- Experience the ongoing forgiveness and cleansing of Jesus (1 John 1:9)
- Observe the fruit of the Spirit being produced in our lives as a result (Galatians 5:16–25)

Nurture in This Guide

After the Scripture readings and articles we've included each week, the conversation will turn toward our hearts. Not only will we look at content, we'll look at how that content profoundly challenges, changes, and confronts you. This will be done through questions, examples, and specific exercises to build these nurture conversations that will continue after this guide.

Act

Led by the Holy Spirit, the group will listen and obey as He calls us to bear fruit in keeping with repentance. The goal is to empower the hands so that in light of his or her repentance each person knows what to do and whom to tell every time the group meets.

Act primarily involves discipling the hands. Once we've discovered the truth about who God is and what He's done, repented of our sin/unbelief, and renewed our faith in Jesus, we need to ask the Spirit to guide us in changing the way we live. Our repentance must have some practical impact on our lives.

When John the Baptist was baptizing people, preparing them for the arrival of the Messiah, he exhorted them to "bear fruit in keeping with repentance," meaning "demonstrate through your life that your repentance is legitimate."

This was a part of Paul's message, as well. As he was telling the story of his conversion to King Agrippa, Paul said, I ". . . declared first to those in Damascus, then in Jerusalem and throughout all the region of Judea, and also to the Gentiles, that they should repent and turn to God, performing deeds in keeping with their repentance" (Acts 26:20 ESV).

Legalism has left a bad taste in the mouths of so many followers of Jesus that talk of works and actions can sometimes be dismissed. While the "you-are-what-you-do" mindset has certainly caused a great deal of damage in the church, the New Testament clearly calls us to change our behavior in light of the gospel.

The book of Titus is one clear example. Titus 2:11–12 (NIV) says, "For the grace of God has appeared that offers salvation to all people. It teaches us to say 'No' to ungodliness and worldly passions, and to live self-controlled, upright and godly lives in this present age. . . ." Experiencing God's grace motivates us to say "no" to sinful actions and "yes" to godly actions!

If the Spirit leads someone to repentance, either outside of the group or during the weekly meeting, spend five-to-ten minutes praying and listening together. Ask the Spirit to speak. Be quiet and listen, waiting for Him to answer two specific questions:

1. What do you want me to do?
2. Who do you want me to tell?

Act in This Guide

Each week, we'll suggest activities, next steps, or questions to help your group walk in obedience. Each of these suggestions offers equipping and a pattern for your community to follow. Don't forget to ask about what happened the previous week as people walked in obedience before you dive into the next week of material.

Transformation Together

Many would say Jesus was the greatest man who ever lived, regardless of their religious affiliation. The word "Christian" means "little Christ," as in one who seeks to walk in the ways of Jesus. But anyone who wants to be more like Him is undoubtedly confronted with a harsh reality: Many changes need to occur if we are to resemble the amazing man Jesus Christ. The concept of change is not foreign to us. Right now, there are probably several things about yourself you'd like to change. But change also raises many questions:

Why should I change? What needs to change? How do I go about changing? Why is change so difficult?

We developed *Growing in Christ Together* to help address those questions and to help you lead a small community of people (DNA group) toward lasting change.

HOW TO USE

Growing in Christ Together

Each week when you meet, *Growing in Christ Together* will help set a basic pattern for your time together. The leader of the group will walk you through the discussion. There is some variation, but roughly the same elements are involved each week:

Notes: A place to jot down notes and thoughts from the discussion or to process through the exercise.

Big Picture: This is a place for you to summarize in a few lines what you learned each week.

Discover: A short passage of scripture to read and discuss and an article to read that will help your group lay the proper foundation for a sustainable DNA group. These articles are taken from a variety of authors. Some leaders encourage everyone to read the articles beforehand, and others find it helpful to read the articles again and out loud together each week. This is something to discuss as you begin your group.

Nurture: Following the readings, the leader will guide a discussion from the content toward our hearts. This is a time directed toward how we respond to God and how the gospel is good news to us.

Act: To ensure that discipleship gets lived out day to day, you'll leave with something to think about or do before your next meeting.

Pray Together: DNA groups always pray together, but occasionally this element will appear calling you to a specific prayer focus. This can be especially helpful for new groups.

Later This Week: Each week we've suggested something to do, think about, pray about, or read when the group isn't together. We also suggest passages of Scripture to read each day between meetings, too.

This Week's Scripture Reading: From week two onward, you'll be challenged toward daily Bible readings first through the book of Ephesians, then select Psalms, passages from the Gospel of Luke, passages from Acts, and lastly the letter of Jude. This is designed to help everyone develop the habit of learning and listening to the Spirit through Scripture.

Leader's Note

The Leader's Guide contains time markers for each element, as well as a few additional elements not found in the participant's guide. Each week, you'll get some extra guidance with headings such as "Opening," "Discover," and "Big Picture." This last one helps you know the most important points to highlight each week. It will help keep the discussion focused.

Notes:

Logistics to Think Through

Here are some things to keep in mind each time you meet:

- Be wise about your meeting place. A coffee shop can work for some groups, but it may not give you the privacy you'll need for honest conversation. Meeting in a home or the quiet corner of a larger public space may be better options.
- You're going to be doing some writing throughout this process. You can use your own journal or the participant's guide that's provided for you. Make sure you have a Bible with you, too.
- You'll be scheduling additional times together, so bring some sort of calendar to each meeting (phone, laptop, paper, a pen for writing on your hand, etc.).

Leader Expectations

There are some expectations unique to the leader of the DNA group:

- Pray consistently for the people in your group. Come with a sense of where the Spirit wants you to go.
- Prepare by reading though the material before your meeting. Come with a sense of where the discussion needs to go. Keep the discussion focused. The Big Picture will help you discern this along with your relationship with the people in your community.
- The Leader's Guide is not top secret. You might want to have the people in your group take turns leading toward the end of the process.

VIDEO: Abe Mysenburg trains on leading a DNA group in this two-part video series.
https://saturatetheworld.com/dna-resources/

WEEK 1

Stories

Week 1

Leader's Note

Set aside at least two hours for this first session as you'll need extra time to read the story and share your own stories. Check out Appendix 3: "Engaging Personal Stories in DNA Groups" to lead this time effectively.

Instructions

Please read "Telling Your Story with Jesus as the Hero" and "Engaging Personal Stories in DNA Groups" located in the Appendix. Come prepared to this week's DNA meeting ready to share vulnerably and listen well. If you run out of time on this first week, have the leader share his/her story, then choose someone to share theirs the next time you meet.

Big Picture

This is where we're going—the big ideas to understand more deeply this week.

› The Bible is made up of one big, overarching story.

› Humans were created in God's image to be like Him, but everyone has rebelled against God.

› God has a plan for restoring everyone and everything to the way He originally created it to be.

› It is all God's work to do this restoration.

Opening [10 minutes]

Take a few minutes to see how each of you is doing and encourage each other. Be careful; this time can easily get away from you.

Setup [2 minutes]

All of our lives are made up of a series of stories. Some of them are true (or seem true to us), and some parts of our stories are caught up in false realities. But there is a big Story that actually helps us make sense of our lives and why things work the way they do in the world. It's called the Story of God. It's a story found throughout the Bible, and it tells of an amazing God who created a perfect world full of beauty, love, and amazing possibilities. The story we're about to read is not a direct quote; it is a summary of the narrative arc of the whole Bible. It will quickly give us the big picture on what God is up to and what life is all about.

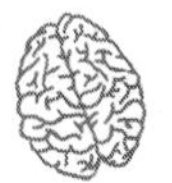

Discover

The Story of God Summary [2 minutes]

> **Leader's Note**
>
> You will read this and tell this story orally. Ask the other participants to put down their pens, Bibles, and participation guides. Allow them to imagine and enter the story.

This is a story found in the Bible about God, a being who has always existed and is the creator of EVERYTHING. God is the only one in this story who always does what is good, right, and perfect; the Bible calls Him holy. While God created the foundations of the earth, angels (His first creation) were there watching. They sang together and worshiped God . . . but some of these angels rebelled against God and His ways. The Bible teaches that all rebellion against God is called sin. Because of God's holiness, He will not allow sin to remain in His presence, so He sent the rebellious angels, now known as demons, down into darkness on the earth.

Then God decided to create another being, called humans, in His own image. God said, "Let us make man in our image to be like us." He then prepared the earth as a place for the humans to live—filling the earth with plants, birds, fish, and animals of all kinds. God created the first humans, Adam and Eve, and placed them in a beautiful garden and trusted them to care for and rule over all of His creation on earth.

God lived closely with these first humans, spending time with them daily, showing them how to live life in the best possible way. They lived their life close to God and under His protection—a life that was full and complete and eternal.

Unfortunately, Adam and Eve chose to rebel against God and His authority, choosing to live in their own ways instead of His. Since God will not allow evil and rebellion to remain in His presence, Adam and Eve were sent out of the garden, away from God. Separated from God and no longer following His ways, Adam and Eve were now subject to sickness, pain, and death. God told them, "The way you have chosen to live will bring you great struggles and pain, and then you will return to the ground from which you came." Not only were these humans now separated from God because of their sin, but they would also suffer death as they were separated from the giver of life.

After leaving the garden the number of humans on earth grew rapidly. Not only did sin spread from Adam and Eve to their sons—it spread from generation to generation.

Even though humans were created in God's image, everyone chose to disobey God. They all constantly acted out in violence against one another. This went on for thousands of years.

Then God established a special relationship and a covenant promise—representing the deepest of all agreements—with a man named Abraham. God told Abraham, "I'll make you the father of a great nation and famous throughout history. I will bless those who bless you and curse those who curse you. The entire earth will be blessed through your descendants. I will always be your God, and you will always be my people."

Abraham's family, called the Israelites, were to be a new kind of people who would show the world what it means once again to live in God's ways. God gave them a vast amount of land where they enjoyed His blessings as they grew into a large nation.

As time went on, the Israelites began doing what was right in their own eyes and rebelled against God and His laws. They stopped trusting in God and worshiped idols—people, things, wealth, and power—instead of God. In their rebellion, the Israelites faced great struggles and ended up a defeated nation of slaves. However God continued to love His people and promised that one day a descendant of theirs would come to rescue and restore humanity and all of creation back to the way God originally created it.

Then there were 400 years of silence between God and His people. The Israelites, called Jews, had been under the control of other nations for hundreds of years. They were now ruled by Rome, the most powerful empire the world had ever known.

Finally God sent an angel to a young woman named Mary in the town of Nazareth. The angel appeared to her and said, "You will become pregnant and have a son, and you are to name Him Jesus. He will become a king whose kingdom will never end! This will happen supernaturally by God's Spirit, so this baby will be called God's Son."

God revealed to Mary and her soon-to-be-husband, Joseph, that this boy was the long-awaited Messiah king, the one whom God promised He'd send to rescue His people! Sure enough the next year, Mary gave birth to a son whom she named Jesus, which means "the God who saves." Jesus grew up in both height and wisdom and was loved by God and everyone who knew Him. He lived a remarkable life, always choosing to live in God's ways and do what was good, right, and perfect.

As a man, Jesus called people to follow Him, inviting them to be a part of what He called the Kingdom of God and calling people once again to live under

God's rule and reign. He said, "God blesses those who realize their need for Him; the humble and poor, the gentle and merciful—the Kingdom of God belongs to them. God blesses the pure in heart and those who hunger and thirst to be with Him." He taught people that the Kingdom of God is within our hearts.

He said, "God showed His great love for people by sending me—His only son—to this world. Anyone who believes in me and lives in my ways will find life that is complete and eternal! He sent me here to save people, not to judge them. Those who want to live in sin and darkness will reject me and bring God's judgment on themselves. Those who want to live in God's ways will trust me and live forever!"

As God promised, He sent Jesus to rescue humanity from sin and the penalty of death. God accepted Jesus' perfect life in place of our own. Jesus was brutally beaten and died painfully on a wooden cross, taking the punishment that all of rebellious humanity deserved! Three days later Jesus conquered death when God raised Him back to life, and He was seen by more than 500 eyewitnesses.

Soon afterward, Jesus went to be with His Father in heaven, rising into the clouds right before His followers' eyes! He promised He would send His own Holy Spirit to come and dwell within them. The Spirit would remind them of all Jesus taught, transform their hearts to be like Jesus, and give them power to walk in the ways of God as Jesus did. Jesus also sent His followers to go out and tell others about Him—His life and His sacrifice for their sins— and lead them to trust Him and walk in His ways.

This was the beginning of what the Bible calls the Church, a community of people all over the world who, because of Jesus, once again enjoy a life that is full and complete, living in the ways of God.

We can join this amazing story. The story continues with us!

The Bible also tells us the end of this story. Jesus promised to come back one day to destroy all evil, sin, and rebellion. Then there will be no more sickness, pain, or death. God's Kingdom will come in fullness, and everyone and everything will live under His rule. Until then, we get to live in God's ways, giving people a foretaste of what life is like in Jesus' Kingdom.

Leader's Note

Read the story out loud a second time. It may seem odd to read it again, but it helps tremendously in our understanding and retention. After all, it is the story of the whole Bible in just a couple pages—it's packed with good stuff!

Nurture [20 minutes]

1. What are some of the indicators that God is the hero and the main character of this story?
2. This Story of God really includes all of our stories too. Where do you see yourself in this Story? Can you see how our stories are really about God?
3. As we have seen in this story, regardless of our rebellion, God's plans cannot be thwarted. Where in your life have you experienced God rescue you from a self-inflicted bad situation?
4. God created us in His image to be like Him and to live a life close to Him. From what you saw in the Story, what would have to change for your life to line up with God's intentions for you? Have you ever tried making those changes on your own? How did that go?

Did you know that God wants to change those things in you? He wants to make you like Jesus.

That is what discipleship is all about: letting God bring about change in our lives from the inside out so we look more like Jesus.

Act [30 minutes]

Now let's share our own life stories with each other (about ten minutes each) and see where our lives really do (or don't) line up with God's story.

Later This Week [10 minutes]

Make plans to do something fun together in the next two weeks. Get together outside of this weekly meeting to do pretty much anything you enjoy that will allow you to interact a lot and have fun together.

Wrap it Up [5 minutes]

Briefly review what you learned today. Jot down the big-picture ideas in your own words. Discuss any final questions. Pray together.

Notes:

WEEK 2

The Four Questions

Week 2

Big Picture

- Learning how to read the Scriptures
- Laying the foundation for ongoing learning about God in our discipleship journey
- The Bible is God-centered

Opening [10 minutes]

Take a few minutes to see how each of you is doing and encourage each other. Be careful, as this time can easily get away from you. If you didn't have time for everyone to share their story last week, dive right in with anyone who is left.

Setup [2 minutes]

Last week, we looked at the true Story of God. In it, we saw that the story of the Bible is completely about God. Humans have roles, but the star of the story is God. Often we look to the Bible as if it's a list of rules for us to follow, or we think it is about us, teaching us the best way to be organized or the best way to help others. Actually, the Bible isn't about us. Each page, paragraph, and phrase is about who God is and what He has done. Many times we are uninspired by our reading of the Bible because we're using it like a manual, not as an inspired book by God, about God, and for us to understand God and His ways. Today we're going to look at four simple questions that help us understand God and grow in our love for God through listening to the Bible.

Discover

Leader's Note

This week you'll begin with an article and then move toward the Scriptures in the "Act" portion.

Article: The Four Questions

Each time we read the Bible we can come to it, depending on the Holy Spirit to teach us and shape us. John 14:26 (ESV) says:

"But the Helper, the Holy Spirit, whom the Father will send in my name, he will teach you all things and bring to your remembrance all that I have said to you."

The Spirit teaches us all things and brings to mind all Jesus said. In other words, when we come to the Bible the Spirit (who inspired each word) is teaching and reminding us of the gospel. How do we engage that process? These simple four questions have proved crucial in helping people see, understand, and remember the gospel as we read the Bible.

1. Who is God?

What does the text say about the character and nature of God? The Bible is God's story—Father, Son, Spirit—so we begin by asking about how His character and nature are revealed in what we're reading. The story is about Him! Look for specific references to His attributes: holy, eternal, all-powerful, all-knowing, ever-present, unchanging, compassionate, gracious, patient, loving, kind, good, gentle, etc. In narrative portions, look for implied references to His attributes. What does the story reveal about His character and nature as Father, Son, and Spirit?

2. What Has He Done?

What does the text say about the work of God? God's work throughout all of human history is diverse and magnificent. All of it is worth proclaiming! However, the person and work of Jesus is revealed on every page of the Bible (Luke 24:27). He is the hero and the main character. The Spirit does not want us to miss Jesus!

Look for references to the life, death, and resurrection of Jesus, either through foreshadowing (saving Noah in the flood, redeeming Israel from slavery in Egypt, King David as a man after God's own heart), through prophecy (Psalm 22, Isaiah 53), or through the New Testament story of Jesus' earthly life and the establishment of His church. This ensures a uniquely Christian, gospel-centered answer to this question.

3. Who Are We in Light of That Truth?

What does the text say about our identity? God has always been working to save "a people for His own possession" (1 Peter 2:9 ESV). Throughout the Bible, note the things that are true of God's people. This adds depth and richness to our understanding of who we are as New Covenant believers. For example, the Levitical priests were anointed and set apart for special service to God. Now we are all anointed with God's Spirit (2 Cor. 1:21–22) and, because of Jesus, are all part of God's "royal priesthood," set apart for special service to God.

4. How Do We Live in Light of That Truth?

How does this change the way we live? When reading the Bible, we almost always start with the question, "How does this apply to my life?" But rightly motivated, gospel-centered action flows out of an understanding of who God is, what He's done, and who we are in light of God's character and work. Rather than starting with this question, end with it.

Then take action! Jesus warns against being merely a hearer of His word but not a doer (Mt. 7:24–27). The gospel motivates and empowers us to live in an entirely new way.

Nurture [20 minutes]

1. What keeps you from reading and exploring the Bible to discover God?
2. How does this method of reading the Bible compare to the way you read the Bible?
3. What would it look like to catch a glimpse of God's character and action on each page of the Bible?

Act [30 minutes]

Try this out together. Spend the next twenty minutes reading Ephesians 1:1–2:10 together and walking through each question. Make a list of answers under each question. Don't settle for a few answers. Search for the truth of the gospel as intensely as a deer searching for water. Who is God, according to this passage? What has He done, according to this passage? Who are we? How do we live?

Don't do this like a homework assignment. Allow yourselves to encourage each other and to respond to the truth you're learning.

After you've walked through the questions, pray for each other to grow in faith and in faithfulness to the things God has called us to remember and to live.

Later This Week [10 minutes]

Begin the Bible reading plan for the rest of this guide. Discuss how you will share what you're learning each day with each other.

Isaiah 6

The point isn't to create a new law to make sure everyone reads their Bible, but attempt to make a plan to grow in understanding the gospel together through listening to the Scriptures.

Wrap it Up [5 minutes]

Briefly review what you learned today. Jot down the big-picture ideas in your own words. Discuss any final questions. Pray together.

This Week's Scripture Reading

As you read, ask the four questions slowly and prayerfully, and remember the context. This is a letter from Paul writing to a church and believers like us to remind them of who God is, what He has done, who we are, and how we live.

- Day 1: Ephesians 2:11–13
- Day 2: Ephesians 2:14–16
- Day 3: Ephesians 2:17–18
- Day 4: Ephesians 2:19–22
- Day 5: Ephesians 3:1–6
- Day 6: Ephesians 3:7–10

Notes:

WEEK 3

The Two Sons

Week 3

Big Picture

This is where we're going—the big ideas to understand more deeply this week.

- Dive into the story of the prodigal sons and deepen our understanding of the gospel's message to us
- Understanding the grace God extends

Opening [10 minutes]

Take a few minutes to see how each of you is doing and encourage each other. Be careful, as this time can easily get away from you. Make sure you talk about the "later this week" from the last time you got together: What was it like to read the Bible with others? How was the accountability? What did you learn about God? How is He leading you to understand your identity?

Setup [1 minute]

The gospel has been compared to a pool shallow enough for a toddler to wade but deep enough for an elephant to swim. It's both simple and profound, affecting those with young faith or mature faith. The Story of God we read last week is the grand redemptive story of the gospel. One of the stories Jesus told that most vividly captures the heart of the gospel is found in Luke 15. Let's take a look at it together.

Discover

Read [20 minutes]

Jesus continued, "There was a man who had two sons. The younger one said to his father, 'Father, give me my share of the estate.' So he divided his property between them.

"Not long after that, the younger son got together all he had, set off for a distant country and there squandered his wealth in wild living. After he had spent everything, there was a severe famine in that whole country, and he began to be in need. So he went and hired himself out to a citizen of that country, who sent him to his fields to feed pigs. He longed to fill his stomach with the pods that the pigs were eating, but no one gave him anything.

Rock Bottom

"When he came to his senses, he said, 'How many of my father's hired men have food to spare, and here I am starving to death! I will set out and go back to my father and say to him: Father, I have sinned against heaven and against you. I am no longer worthy to be called your son; make me like one of your hired men.' So he got up and went to his father.

"But while he was still a long way off, his father saw him and was filled with compassion for him; he ran to his son, threw his arms around him and kissed him.

"The son said to him, 'Father, I have sinned against heaven and against you. I am no longer worthy to be called your son. "But the father said to his servants, 'Quick! Bring the best robe and put it on him. Put a ring on his finger and sandals on his feet. Bring the fattened calf and kill it. Let's have a feast and celebrate. For this son of mine was dead and is alive again; he was lost and is found.' So they began to celebrate.

"Meanwhile, the older son was in the field. When he came near the house, he heard music and dancing. So he called one of the servants and asked him what was going on. 'Your brother has come,' he replied, 'and your father has killed the fattened calf because he has him back safe and sound.'

"The older brother became angry and refused to go in. So his father went out and pleaded with him. But he answered his father, 'Look! All these years I've

been slaving for you and never disobeyed your orders. Yet you never gave me even a young goat so I could celebrate with my friends. But when this son of yours who has squandered your property with prostitutes comes home, you kill the fattened calf for him!'

"'My son,' the father said, 'you are always with me, and everything I have is yours. But we had to celebrate and be glad, because this brother of yours was dead and is alive again; he was lost and is found.'" —Luke 15:11–32 (NIV)

Nurture [20 minutes]

At the beginning of the story, the younger son demands his inheritance, which is like saying to his dad, "I wish you were dead!"

What do you think the younger son really wants in life?
What his will wants, not his fathers.

Think about the older son's conversation with the father. He says, "I've been slaving for you all these years. Where's my party?!" If he considered his work to be like slavery, why do you think he kept at it? What do you think he wanted in life? Grace

Do you think either son truly loved the father and wanted to be with him?

Their actions look very different, but explain how both sons' hearts are very similar.

Leader's Note

Both sons wanted the father's stuff and not the father. The older brother tried to earn his father's favor through hard work.

Why doesn't the father punish the younger son? What does the father say to the older brother at the end of the story?

This parable of the lost sons is a picture of what is called the gospel.

After hearing this story, how would you explain the gospel?

Act [10 minutes]

Which son do you identify with in this story? What does the father do toward you? How is God inviting you to respond?

What would it look like to obey this parable? If you're an "older brother," how will you respond to the Father? If you're a "younger brother," how will you return to the Father?

What can you do this week to enter the feast and party that is prepared for you?

Later This Week [10 minutes]

Plan a time to hang out together and do something everyone enjoys or might enjoy. Chose something that allows you casually to pursue deeper relationship with each other outside of any structured time.

Wrap it Up [5 minutes]

Jot down a few big ideas or areas of obedience you need to take as you walk away from this meeting. Pray as you engage the world and ask God for wisdom in seeing and having compassion for the "older" and "younger" brothers in your life.

This Week's Scripture Reading

As you read, ask the four questions slowly and prayerfully and remember the context. This is a letter from Paul writing to a church and believers like us to remind them of who God is, what He has done, who we are, and how we live.

- Day 1: Ephesians 3:11–13
- Day 2: Ephesians 3:14–19
- Day 3: Ephesians 3:20–21
- Day 4: Ephesians 4:1–3
- Day 5: Ephesians 4:4–6
- Day 6: Ephesians 4:7–10

Notes:

WEEK 4

The Gospel

Week 4

Big Picture

- Clarify the nature of the gospel
- Introduce the relationship between the gospel and discipleship

Opening [10 minutes]

Take a few minutes to see how each of you is doing and encourage each other. Be careful, as this time can easily get away from you! Ask questions about how each person engaged and responded to the story of the two sons last week.

Setup [2 minutes]

The word "gospel" or phrase "good news" rolls off our tongues in Christians circles, but what does it mean? What are the implications of this phrase? We're tempted to pretend we know everything about the "gospel" and stay away from questions about it that may seem obvious. However, the gospel is so profound, no one can fully grasp the magnitude of God's rescue and restoration of the world. Today we're asking the question that seems basic but must become daily: "What is the gospel?"

Discover

Read [5 minutes]

Now I would remind you, brothers, of the gospel I preached to you, which you received, in which you stand, and by which you are being saved, if you hold fast to the word I preached to you—unless you believed in vain.

For I delivered to you as of first importance what I also received: that Christ died for our sins in accordance with the Scriptures, that he was buried, that he was raised on the third day in accordance with the Scriptures, and that he appeared to Cephas, then to the twelve. Then he appeared to more than five hundred brothers at one time, most of whom are still alive, though some have fallen asleep. Then he appeared to James, then to all the apostles. Last of all, as to one untimely born, he appeared also to me. For I am the least of the apostles, unworthy to be called an apostle, because I persecuted the church of God. But by the grace of God I am what I am, and his grace toward me was not in vain. On the contrary, I worked harder than any of them, though it was not I, but the grace of God that is with me. Whether then it was I or they, so we preach and so you believed. —1 Corinthians 15:1–11 (ESV)

Pray [10 minutes]

Paul says the gospel is the most important thing in the entire world. Pray for each other asking God to reveal the wonder, majesty, and goodness of the message of Jesus. Spend time confessing your lack of understanding and your desire to know the good news.

Article: What is the Gospel? [10 minutes]

The gospel is called the "good news," and it is particularly good news about our sin problem. In a nutshell, we can sum it up this way:

The gospel is that God Himself has come to rescue and restore creation in and through the work of Jesus Christ on our behalf.

Why does creation (which includes me) need rescuing? Because of sin.

Sin is living for my fame and glory instead of God's. Sin is living life my way, for me, instead of living life, God's way, for God. We have all sinned and really need the gospel—we desperately need Jesus to rescue us from the penalty and effects of sin, which the Bible teaches is ultimate and eternal separation from God. When we repent (change our mind about who is really God in our lives) and by faith we believe that Jesus' life, death, and resurrection has secured our rescue and restored us to a right relationship with God the Father, then this good news is true for us! We also have been sent out to proclaim this same gospel of restoration to the entire world.

Understanding Two Gospel Perspectives

We can read the Bible across the grain (thematically), and we can read it with the grain (as a story). Both are necessary, and each one leads to a different way of seeing the gospel. It takes both perspectives to understand and engage the gospel fully.

1. Thematically

The gospel power. We understand the means of salvation.

God—eternal, all-powerful, creator of everything

Sin—humanity has all chosen self-rule over submission in relationship to God; the penalty for sin is death

Jesus—God incarnate came to die as a substitute for the penalty of humanity's sins

Faith—by faith in what Jesus did, not by any effort of our own, we are saved from our sins.

In this case, the good news is that God is completely aware of our sin problem and in and through the work of Jesus Christ accepts us AND changes us by the power of His Spirit. We have been saved from the penalty of sin (justification), are being saved from the power of sin (sanctification), and will be saved from the presence of sin. This means the same power that saved us from the penalty for sin also helps us obey God now.

This results in my understanding that . . .

I am more broken and sinful than I ever dared believe, and at the same time I am more loved and accepted than I ever dared hope because of Jesus.

2. As a Story

The gospel purpose. Here we come to know the reason for salvation. We can look at the gospel through the lens of a story.

Creation ▶ Fall ▶ Redemption ▶ Restoration

In this case, the good news is that God sent His Son to redeem the world from the effects of sin and create a new humanity. Eventually the whole world will be renewed to the way God originally created it. Rebellion, death, decay, injustice, and suffering will all be removed. When everything is restored, God will be seen by all for who He truly is—He will be glorified.

How does this happen? Jesus helped clarify how we accomplish the purpose of the gospel by giving us His mission: “Go and make disciples” (Matthew 28:19). A disciple of Jesus is someone who is learning to apply the gospel to absolutely every part of life. As the arts, industry, politics, families—all areas of culture—are being filled with Jesus’ disciples bringing about His gospel restoration, the earth is being filled with His glory! That is the point of the restoration of all things—that God would be glorified!

The gospel is not just about my individual happiness or God’s plan for my life. The gospel is about God’s plan for the world.

Good News!

When we repent of our sin (view it as God does) and receive the forgiveness and new life that Jesus has offered us, we begin a journey of restoration inside and out as disciples of Jesus. Being a disciple is not primarily learning a bunch of information or maintaining certain spiritual disciplines. Discipleship is not a class or a program you go through. Becoming like Jesus is all about the gospel. A disciple of Jesus is someone who is learning to apply the gospel to absolutely every part of life. The life of a disciple requires allowing the truth of the gospel to sink deep into our hearts, transforming our passions and motivations that in turn radically rearranges how we live. Although we have a role to play, the Holy Spirit is the one who does this transforming work.

This gospel restoration happens in us in the context of a community on Jesus' mission, and it's not just for us—but for the entire world!

Nurture [15 minutes]

Explain in your own words the two perspectives on the gospel.

How do you understand HOW we are saved? How do you understand WHY we are saved?

How does Jesus' command to make disciples help us be a preview of the complete restoration Jesus will one day usher in?

As you are led through this gospel DNA process, begin praying and thinking even now about who you will lead through it when you are done. Who might those people be?

We often tend to think of the gospel in individualistic terms. How is community or family important to the purpose of the gospel? What simple steps can you commit to taking to live more like family with the others in this DNA group?

Act [10 minutes]

Think of a specific friend or neighbor who does not know Jesus. Imagine he or she asked you, "I've heard you and your friends use the word 'gospel' a lot. Can you tell me what you mean by that?" In light of what you've learned last week and today, how would you explain the gospel to this person if you only had two minutes for this first conversation?

Later This Week [5 minutes]

Think about this for next time: We defined a disciple as "someone who is learning to apply the gospel to absolutely every part of life." What is one specific area of your life where you are not yet applying the gospel fully? Where is there a need for restoration in your life? If you had to pick one thing to start with, trusting God to make the change in your life, what would that be?

Do whatever you need to do to remind yourself to think about this question this week. Put it in your calendar, write a note, put it where you'll see it often, etc.

Wrap it Up [5 minutes]

Briefly review what you learned today. Jot down the big-picture ideas in your own words. Discuss any final questions. Pray together.

This Week's Scripture Reading

As you read, ask the four questions slowly and prayerfully and remember the context. This is a letter from Paul writing to a church and believers like us to remind them of who God is, what He has done, who we are, and how we live.

- Day 1: Ephesians 4:11–13
- Day 2: Ephesians 4:14–16
- Day 3: Ephesians 4:17–20
- Day 4: Ephesians 4:21–24
- Day 5: Ephesians 4:25–32
- Day 6: Ephesians 5:1–2

Notes:

WEEK 5

Change

Week 5

Big Picture

- God's singular purpose for us is that we become like Jesus
- Prayer is crucial to discipleship
- Identify a specific area of life we will bring the gospel to bear on for the next few months

Opening [5 minutes]

Take a few minutes to see how each of you is doing and encourage each other. Be careful, as this time can easily get away from you. At the beginning, you normally talk about the "later this week" from the last time you got together, but today you'll have a lot of time for that at the end.

Setup [10 minutes]

What is success to you? Don't discuss the definitions from your culture, society, or friends, but your personal definition of success in life.

Leader's Note

Lead your DNA partners toward a definition like "finding what God wants me to do and doing it" or "glorifying God" or "becoming more like Jesus." God should be the one who determines what success is for us. You may want to ask a follow-up question like, "Where does God fit into all this?" or "How do you think the Bible might define success?"

Discover [5 minutes]

But when you pray, go into your room, close the door and pray to your Father, who is unseen. Then your Father, who sees what is done in secret, will reward you. And when you pray, do not keep on babbling like pagans, for they think they will be heard because of their many words. Do not be like them, for your Father knows what you need before you ask him. This, then, is how you should pray:

Our Father in heaven, hallowed be your name,
your kingdom come, your will be done,
on earth as it is in heaven.
Give us today our daily bread.
And forgive us our debts,
as we also have forgiven our debtors.
And lead us not into temptation,
but deliver us from the evil one.
—Matthew 6:6–13 (NIV)

Pray Together [15 minutes]

Prayer is a vital part of the life of a disciple. Spend some time praying together as a group before you continue. Ask the Spirit to give you wisdom as you discuss becoming like Jesus today. Remember—prayer is simply a conversation between the Father and His kids. There's no need to sound impressive or rehearsed. We're invited to come boldly, so say what's on your heart. You can use Jesus' prayer to guide you if you'd like.

Article: What Would You Like to Change? [10 minutes]

We learned from the Story of God that humans were made in God's image. We reflected His image or His glory like a mirror. But when we rebelled against God, that image was broken. The Bible tells us, "All have sinned and fall short of the glory of God" (Romans 3:23 NIV). The mirror has been shattered. We reflect a distorted image. Ephesians 4:22 (NIV) calls this our "old self" or our flesh:

You were taught, with regard to your former way of life, to put off your old self, which is being corrupted by its deceitful desires.

We can't be the people we want to be, let alone the people we were made to be.

We also learned in the Story that Jesus reflected God's image perfectly. Colossians 1:15 (CSB) says, "He is the image of the invisible God." Hebrews 1:3 (NIV) says He is "the radiance of God's glory and the exact representation of His being." Jesus said, "Anyone who has seen me has seen the Father" (John 14:9 NIV).

Just as humans were designed to do in the beginning, Jesus shows the world what God is like. He does it perfectly, and John eloquently highlights the reality of Jesus's fullness in the opening lines of his gospel in John 1:14 (NIV):

The Word became flesh and made his dwelling among us. We have seen his glory, the glory of the One and Only Son, who came from the Father, full of grace and truth.

Jesus is the glory of the Father. He makes God known in the world. He is God in human form. He shows us what it means to be the image of God and to reflect God's glory. That's why the New Testament sometimes says we should be like God and sometimes says we should be like Christ. It's because Christ is the true image of God.

Jesus shows us God's agenda for change. God isn't interested in making us religious. Think of Jesus, who was hated by religious people. God isn't interested in making us "spiritual," if by spiritual we mean detached: Jesus was God getting stuck in. God isn't interested in making us self-absorbed: Jesus was self-giving personified. God isn't interested in serenity: Jesus was passionate for God, was angry at sin, and wept for the city. The word "holy" means set apart from or different from our sinful ways. It didn't mean being set apart from the world but being consecrated to God in the world. He was God's glory in and for the world.

The word "glory" means "weight," as in "a person of importance, a weighty person." So Jesus shows us the full weight, the full significance, of the character and nature of God. Jesus shows us God as He really is. God, in all of His majesty, splendor, wisdom, beauty, power, compassion, grace, patience, and love, was put on display in the person of Jesus Christ.

Through Jesus' life, He demonstrated power over death and demons. His compassionate heart led Him to preach the good news to the poor and to heal the sick. Through Jesus' death and resurrection, we see God's glory even more clearly. Jesus willingly took all of the sins of humanity and piled them on His shoulders, becoming sin (2 Corinthians 5:21). He endured the wrath of God against the sin of humanity and prayed, "Father, forgive them." But death couldn't hold Him, and He overcame the sentence that all humanity had faced since the garden. Jesus is the image of the invisible God!

Because of our connection to Jesus, we are now being restored to our original Image, the Image of Christ. Colossians 3:9–10 (NIV) says, "Do not lie to each other, since you have taken off your old self [There's that same idea again.] with its practices and have put on the new self, which is being renewed in knowledge in the image of its Creator."

Our original identity as image-bearers of God has been completely restored through the work of Jesus on our behalf. We reflect His image with greater and greater clarity as we live the life Jesus modeled for us and produces in us through His Spirit. It's as if the broken mirror is being healed and is slowly reflecting an accurate image again.

This process—us becoming more like Jesus so we reflect more accurately what God is like—is the number-one thing God is always up to in our lives.

For those God foreknew He also predestined to be conformed to the likeness (or image) of His Son, that he might be the firstborn among many brothers (Romans 8:29).

What this means is that God had a plan before time began to mold and shape you into the image of His Son Jesus. He uses both blessings and trials to do that shaping work. Therefore, we should submit to His perfect work in us. The Story is about Him!

From God's perspective, becoming like Jesus is the goal of the entire Christian life. The purpose of our lives is to bring glory to God, to show the world what He's like as His image-bearers. To do that, we must be conformed into the image of His Son, which brings Him glory! As we become like Christ, we will bring glory to God.

Again, a disciple is someone who is learning to apply the gospel to absolutely every part of life. Discipleship is all about letting God bring about change in our lives from the inside out so we look more like Jesus.

Nurture [10 minutes]

In your own words, describe how Jesus reflects the glory of God.

In Romans 8:28, what is the "good" God works all things together for?

What do you think it means that God "predestined us to be conformed to the likeness of his Son"?

Second Corinthians 5:17 says we are a new creation. How are you a "new creation"?

Do you want to be like Jesus? Why or why not?

Act: Gospel Change Project [20 minutes]

Remember that a disciple is someone learning to apply the gospel to absolutely every part of life. Throughout the next several weeks, you will get to allow the gospel to change you in a specific area, making you more like Jesus one degree at a time. Many discussions with your DNA partners will be about bringing the gospel to bear on this specific area, which we'll call your gospel change project. The next time around you can easily use this same guide and focus on a different gospel change project as you lead others.

What specific area of your life, actions, and attitudes would you like to change?

Take some time right now to pray and ask God to reveal to you what area He wants each of us to work on.

Here's some help:

Think of an area of your life that you would like to change. It might be a behavior (such as lying or getting drunk or inappropriate relationships), or it might be an emotion (such as getting bitter or angry).

Is your gospel change project about changing your behavior or emotions?

It is no good choosing change in someone else. For example, you cannot choose having better behaved children or having a better marriage. You must choose something about you. For example, you might choose not shouting at my children or not getting irritated by my spouse.

Is your gospel change project about something specific? Try not to choose something too general such as being a better parent. Choose a specific behavior or a specific emotion. It should be specific enough for you to be able to remember the last time you did it or felt it.

Is there something in your life you're kind of embarrassed to bring up right now? It's not making you happy, and you know it's not making God happy. That's probably the thing the Spirit's bringing to mind for you to work on to be more conformed to the likeness of Jesus.

Share with each other the area of life the Spirit is bringing to mind, and write it down.

Leader's Note

Don't move on through this guide without everyone identifying a specific area of life for the gospel change project.

Later This Week

Notice how often this thing you want to change comes up in your life. (You may want to jot down some notes.) How does it affect you? How does it affect others? More importantly, how does this thing you want to change make you look less like Jesus? Remember the point of gospel change is that we look more and more like Jesus and show the world what He is like. Who and what are people seeing in those moments?

Put in place whatever reminders you need to answer these questions this week.

Wrap it Up [5 minutes]

Briefly review what you learned today. Jot down the big-picture ideas in your own words. Discuss any final questions. Pray together.

This Week's Scripture Reading

As you read, ask the four questions slowly and prayerfully and remember the context. This is a letter from Paul writing to a church and believers like us to remind them of the who God is, what He has done, who we are, and how we live.

- Day 1: Ephesians 5:3–4
- Day 2: Ephesians 5:5–10
- Day 3: Ephesians 5:11–14
- Day 4: Ephesians 5:15–16
- Day 5: Ephesians 5:17–20
- Day 6: Ephesians 5:21–24

Notes:

WEEK 6

Motivation

Week 6

Big Picture

- Becoming like Jesus has more to do with our motivation and affections than merely our behavior—it's about the heart
- We all tend to be motivated wrongly, thinking we can justify ourselves
- The gospel transforms our motivations, and we grow to understand it's not about us—it's about Jesus

Opening [10 minutes]

Take a few minutes to see how each of you is doing and encourage each other. Be careful, as this time can easily get away from you. Make sure you talk about the "later this week" from the last time you got together.

Setup [1 minute]

Bring to mind whatever you decided on for your gospel change project. What do you think is behind that sin in your life? Today we will begin to look at why we often do the very things we don't want to do.

Discover

Read [2 minutes]

Teaching his disciples, Jesus said...

No good tree bears bad fruit, nor does a bad tree bear good fruit. Each tree is recognized by its own fruit. People do not pick figs from thornbushes, or grapes from briers. A good man brings good things out of the good stored up in his heart, and an evil man brings evil things out of the evil stored up in his heart. For the mouth speaks what the heart is full of. —Luke 6:43–45 (NIV)

Pray Together [15 minutes]

Pray together through this passage. You may talk with the Father about some of these questions: Where have you seen good fruit in your life? Bad fruit? What does this reveal about your heart? What's the real problem?

Leader's Note

Be okay with silence and listening. You might want to read the passage, ask the above questions, and then call for everyone to sit silently listening to the Spirit for five minutes before praying the passage together.

Article: Why Would You Like to Change? Part I [10 minutes]

Why do you want to change? Think about it for a minute. Why do you want to be more like Jesus? Most people want to improve on some character issue in their lives, change some behavior. What's motivating you to want to be a more patient or loving person? To be a better wife or father?

While our motives are complex and hard to discern, they can often be boiled down into one of three categories:

1. To Prove Ourselves to God

I don't want God to have to work too hard to accept me. I want to help Him out. I want to be acceptable to God on the basis of my own merit. I want to put Him in a place of obligation, where He must bless me for my hard work.

Deep down, we all want to change so we can justify ourselves, to prove our worth. We are all natural-born legalists, laboring and toiling under the weight of guilt and insecurity. This instinct comes from our pride-filled flesh (also called our sinful nature).

God's grace is an insult to our flesh. We want to be seen by God and others as successful and worthy. We want to pull ourselves up by our own bootstraps. We want to take credit. The reality is that we can do nothing to earn or lose God's love.

All the time God is saying, "In my love I gave my Son for you. He's done everything needed to secure my blessing. I love you as you are and accept you in Him." God cannot love a Christian more than He does now—no matter how much we change our lives. God will not love a Christian less than He does now—no matter what mess we make of our lives.

God demonstrates his own love for us in this: While we were still sinners, Christ died for us. —Romans 5:8 (NIV)

2. To Prove Ourselves to Other People

This is often the reason why I want to change: I want other people to be impressed by me. We may want to fit in or get other people's approval. We certainly don't want other people finding out what we're like inside. We wear masks to hide our real selves from people. Wearing the mask can be a great strain; it's like acting a role all the time. However we dare not let other people see us as we really are.

One of the problems with trying to prove yourself to other people is that it means they set the standard. Their standards may be ungodly, but you adopt their behavior to fit in. Their standards may be ungodly, but you're living in obedience to other people rather than obedience to God. Often what happens is that you settle for living like other people even when that falls short of living like Jesus. Sometimes you measure yourself against other people and decide you are more righteous. Indeed often we point the finger at other people's faults so we can feel better about ourselves. Instead we should be comparing ourselves to Jesus, finding we fall a long way short of God's standards and discovering we desperately need a Savior.

Here's the bottom line: I want other people to be impressed by me. For my entire marriage, I have wanted the approval of my wife. Her opinion has been more weighty in my life than God's. When I know I've hurt her and I know I've not measured up in her eyes as a husband, it's a struggle.

But this doesn't just affect marriage. This desire to prove ourselves to other people affects our work relationships, our friendships, the people we're serving, our parenting, even our relationships with total strangers ("I want these people who I've never met to think well of me.").

We perform to hide our real selves from people. Another way to think about performing is that it's like wearing a mask. We can often be like actors, putting on a false front to impress people or vigorously defending ourselves so we're not seen for who we really are. Many of us know how draining it can be to feel like we're putting on an act all day long! This is a huge cause of stress in our lives.

This desire to prove ourselves to others hinders our growth as disciples because our primary objective is to be like other people—whatever will gain their approval—instead of being like Jesus.

3. To Prove Yourself to Yourself

When we mess up, we might hear things such as "Idiot" or "stupid" or "failure" go through our minds. In the past, I realized that one of my biggest fears in life was letting myself down, failing to live up to my own expectations for myself. I couldn't bear the thought of being labeled, even in my own mind, as a failure.

My ego still takes a serious hit when I mess up. Often the biggest sense of a letdown is having to face myself in the mirror. This means I am viewing my sin as primarily an offense against me.

Justified by Grace

What's wrong with wanting to change so we can prove ourselves to God or other people or ourselves? It does not work. We might fool other people for a while. We might even fool ourselves. But we can never change enough to impress God. Here is the reason. Trying to impress God, others, or ourselves puts us at the center of the change project. It makes change all about me. It's all about making me look good. It is done for my glory. That is sin. In fact that's pretty much the definition of sin. Sin is living for my glory instead of God's glory. Sin is living life my way for me instead of living life God's way for God. Much of the time that means rejecting God as Lord and wanting to be our own lord, but it can also involve rejecting God as Savior and wanting to be our own savior. Pharisees do good works and repent of bad works. But gospel repentance includes repenting of good works done for wrong reasons. John Gerstner says: "The thing that really separates us from God is not so much our sin, but our damnable good works."

Another word for proving ourselves is justify. We want to justify ourselves to God, to show Him we are good enough. We want to justify ourselves to other people or ourselves, to show we are respectable. However we are justified through faith in what Christ has done. When you feel the desire to prove yourself, remember you are justified by Christ. You are accepted by God already because of what Christ has done. You cannot do anything to make yourself more acceptable to God than you already are. You do not need to worry whether other people are impressed by you because you are justified by God. What makes you feel good is not what you have done but what Christ has done for you. Your identity is not dependent on your change. You are a child of the heavenly king.

Deep down in all of us is a tendency to base our acceptance and worth on what we do. In theological terms this is basing justification on sanctification. Religious people do this, but so do most non-religious people. They do a secular version in which their identity is based on their performance. Christians, too, constantly slip back into a religious motivation. We are all trying to be our own savior. We want to make a contribution to our salvation that we can claim at least a little credit for it, but justification is not based on sanctification. We are made right with God entirely at God's initiative and entirely through His grace.

The truth is that it is the other way around: Our sanctification is based on our justification. If we do not grasp the reality of grace, our good works will be done for wrong reasons. Without grace, we view life as a contract between us and God; we do good works, and in return He blesses us. When things go well we are filled with pride. When things go badly we either blame ourselves (which leads to crushing guilt) or we blame God (which leads to anger and bitterness). Only when we grasp God's great love displayed on the cross are we free to serve Him for His own sake.

Here is the real problem with changing to impress. God has given His Son for us so we can be justified. Jesus died on the cross, separated from His Father, bearing the full weight of God's wrath so we can be accepted by God. When we try to impress by our good works we are saying, in effect, that the cross wasn't enough. "What Jesus did on the cross was all well and good, but I need to finish the job. Jesus didn't quite do enough for me to be accepted by God. I need to do a bit more. I need to atone for myself." "It is finished," Jesus cried. "Not quite," we answer back. "I still need to do this to get God's blessing." Imagine you owed a huge debt that left you languishing in poverty. Then a relative pays off your debt and sets you free. They have given you thousands of dollars—everything that was needed. But then you try to give them some loose change in your pocket as repayment. You want everyone to know you helped pay off the debt, that it was joint effort. It would be pointless and insulting.

You will not cleanse a single sin from your life that you have not first recognized to be pardoned through the cross. If you fail to realize that Jesus has completely paid the penalty for the sin, then you will still work hard on your own to atone for it. You will never be free of the sin if you think it's up to you to pay for it. If you do not see your sin completely pardoned, then your affections, desires, and motives will be wrong. Your aim will be to prove yourself. Your focus will be the consequences of your sin rather than hating the sin itself and desiring God in its place.

Nurture [15 minutes]

Why do you want to change?

Do you think you will miss the sin you give up?

Do you think of giving up your sin as an unpleasant duty you need to do to be accepted by God?

Do you want to change for the wrong reasons?

What evidence is there that you might be trying to prove yourself to God?

What evidence is there that you might be trying to prove yourself to others?

What evidence is there that you might be trying to prove yourself to yourself?

Leader's Note

- Listen for bitterness toward God, entitlement, sense of God's blessing being connected to their obedience, guilt, shame, etc.
- Listen for fear of man, insecurity, comparison, need for approval, jealousy, dishonesty, etc.
- Listen for fear of failure, unwillingness to admit mistakes, pride, etc.

Act [15 minutes]

Take a look at the following paragraphs. We have taken some verses from the Bible and made them say the opposite of what they actually say. Let's see if we can turn them back into what they really say.

When we prove ourselves by living a good life, we have peace with God through what we do. It is what we do that gives us access to God's blessing and a good standing in people's eyes. This means we can worry a bit less about whether we will share God's glory in heaven.

It is by changing that your problems will be sorted out, through working hard. It's up to us. This is what we can do for God. We are saved by what we do, so we can prove ourselves. If we do the good works God plans for us, then we can become God's masterpiece, new people in Christ Jesus.

You can check by looking at Romans 5:1–2 and Ephesians 2:8–10.[1]

If what we talked about today is true, how should it affect my thoughts? How should it affect my passions and motivations? How should it affect my actions? How will we encourage and hold each other accountable to these things?

Later This Week [3 minutes]

Discuss what you are learning with at least one other person outside of this DNA group. Who might that be? Tell them why you most often want to change (to prove yourself to God, others, or yourself). Hold each other accountable to this. Maybe check in with each other during the week with a quick phone call to encourage each other to be faithful.

Leader's Notes

Heads up—next week, you'll need to make some time to hang together as family. Hopefully you're doing that often anyway. Plan ahead if you need to.

Wrap it Up [5 minutes]

Briefly review what you learned today. Jot down the big-picture ideas in your own words. Discuss any final questions. Pray together.

This Week's Scripture Reading

As you read, ask the four questions slowly and prayerfully and remember the context. This is a letter from Paul writing to a church and believers like us to remind them of the who God is, what He has done, who we are, and how we live.

- Day 1: Ephesians 5:25–27
- Day 2: Ephesians 5:28–30
- Day 3: Ephesians 5:31–33
- Day 4: Ephesians 6:1–3
- Day 5: Ephesians 6:4
- Day 6: Ephesians 6:5–8

Notes:

WEEK 7

Identity

Week 7

Big Picture

- We are given a new identity as children of God
- We are called to "be who we are"
- To live out our new identity is to experience joy and delight in God

Opening [10 minutes]

Take a few minutes to see how each of you is doing and encourage each other. Be careful, as this time can easily get away from you. Make sure you talk about the "later this week" from the last time you got together.

Setup [1 minute]

Have you ever asked yourself the questions, "Who am I?" and "Why am I here?" In a sense, we all live each day out of our answers to those questions. The New Testament teaches over and over that we have a new identity because of Jesus. Again and again it calls us to "be who we are." Change is not about achieving something so we can impress. It's about living out the new identity God gives us in Jesus. So who are we?[2]

Discover

Read [15 minutes]

But when the set time had fully come, God sent his Son, born of a woman, born under the law, to redeem those under the law, that we might receive adoption to sonship. Because you are his sons, God sent the Spirit of his Son into our hearts, the Spirit who calls out, "Abba, Father." So you are no longer a slave, but God's child; and since you are his child, God has made you also an heir... It is for freedom that Christ has set us free. Stand firm, then, and do not let yourselves be burdened again by a yoke of slavery... You, my brothers and sisters, were called to be free. But do not use your freedom to indulge the flesh; rather, serve one another humbly in love. —Galatians 4:4-7; 5:1; 5:13 (NIV)

Sons in the Greco-Roman world had legal standing, privilege, and authority that daughters did not. In one sense, whether we are male or female, we are made "sons" of the Father.

Whether your dad was amazing, average, absent, or abusive, think back to the father in the parable of the lost sons as a picture of God who is the perfect father.

What might be some implications of being a son in God's family?

For you personally, for a group of people who are all in this family, for everyone you know who isn't part of this family . . .

Article: Why Would You Like to Change? Part II [10 minutes]

We used to be slaves to sin, says Paul. We were trapped by it. We all know this if we stop to think about. Think about the times you have tried to change but have failed. We cannot be the people we want to be, let alone become people who are like Jesus.

We are also slaves to the law. In Galatians Paul is talking about the law of God given through Moses. But what he says is true of any attempt to change using a set of rules. Instead of setting us free from sin, law crushes us.

God sent His Son to buy our freedom. We are no longer slaves with a slave master. Now we are children with a Father. We do not have to worry about proving ourselves because God says, "You are my child." We do not have to worry about being accepted by God because God has sent His Spirit so that with confidence we can call Him "Abba, Father." (In Aramaic, the language

Jesus spoke, Abba is a respectful and intimate name for a father.) Our identity as sons of God the Father is so central and so pervasive in the gospel that J.I Packer wrote, "You sum up the whole of New Testament teaching in a single phrase, if you speak of it as a revelation of the Fatherhood of the holy Creator. . . . 'Father' is the Christian name for God."[3]

We were slaves of sin, and now we are children of God. It would be crazy to go on living as slaves and not to live as children. Freedom does not mean we can sin. That is not freedom. That is going back into slavery. Imagine an alcoholic whose addiction has wrecked his life. Someone kindly puts him through rehab, and after several months he leaves, free from his addiction. He is not going to say, "I'm free at last so I'm going to get plastered." That is not freedom. That is returning to his old slavery.

When you were slaves to sin, you were free from the obligation to do right. And what was the result? You are now ashamed of the things you used to do, things that end in eternal doom. But now you are free from the power of sin and have become slaves of God. Now you do those things that lead to holiness and result in eternal life. For the wages of sin is death, but the free gift of God is eternal life through Christ Jesus our Lord. —Romans 6:20–23 (NLT)

It was Sophie's first day with her adoptive parents. She stalked nervously around her new home, fearing one of the beatings she used to get if something was broken. The toys in her room went untouched. She could not quite believe they were hers. At dinner she secretly stuffed food in her pocket; you never knew where your next meal would come from when you were on the streets.

That night she felt alone in her big room. She would have cried if she had not long since learned to suppress emotion. Now listen to her new mother one year on: "She crawled into bed with me last night because she was having a bad dream. She curled up next to me, put her head on my chest, told me she loved me, smiled, and went to sleep. I nearly cried with contentment."

Sophie had a new identity on day one. She had become a child in a new family, but she still lived like a child of the street. Her actions and attitudes were shaped by her old identity. Christians too have been adopted into a new family and given a new identity. We are to live out our new identity—to be who we are. Do not live like a slave when you can live like a child of the King of heaven.

Our identity as God's children is the foundation of who we are now because of Jesus. As God's children, we bear His name everywhere we go. We are His family, His church. Church then is not a place or event. It's who we are. Some implications of being family are that we care for one another and live like God is our Father—we are like Him, do what He says, love Him, and know He loves us.

As God's children, we, like Jesus, are sent to the world so others may experience what God is like. We are ministers of reconciliation bearing God's message of reconciliation. As we obey Jesus's command to make disciples, God is using us to reconcile people to Himself. Jesus said, "As the Father has sent me, I am sending you" (John 20:21 NIV). We are missionaries.

So what's the motivation to change and live in this new identity? The reason Christians should want to change is to enjoy the freedom from sin and delight in God that God gives to us through Jesus. I want to highlight four things from this definition.

First, growing in holiness is not a sad, dutiful drudge. It is about joy. It is discovering true joy—the joy of knowing and serving God. There is self-denial—sometimes hard and painful self-denial—but true self-denial leads to gaining your life (Mark 8:34–37).

Second, gospel change is about living in freedom. We stop living as slaves to sin. We refuse to go back to our chains and to our filth. We live in the wonderful freedom God gives us. We are free to be the people we should be.

Third, gospel change is about discovering the delight of knowing and serving God. We give up on our sin and in return we get God Himself! Our job is to stop grubbing around in the dirt and instead to enjoy knowing God. We give up our cheap imitations and enjoy the real thing. We often think of holiness as a means to an end—the end being the approval of God or the admiration of others. Holiness is the end, and the means is God's grace giving Christ for us and the Spirit in us. Our problem is we think of holiness as giving up the pleasures that sin offers for some worthy but drab life. But holiness is recognizing that the pleasures of sin are empty and temporary while all the time God is inviting us to magnificent, true, full, and rich pleasures that last forever.

Fourth, becoming like Jesus is something God gives to us. It is not an achievement we offer to God. It is enjoying the new identity He has given us in Christ. It begins with His work for us. He has set us free from sin and offers a relationship with Himself.

There are two feasts. There is the feast of God, and there is the feast of sin. We are invited to both. God invites us to find satisfaction in Him. Sin entices us with its lies to look for satisfaction in sin. So we are double-booked. All the time we have to choose which feast we attend. We cannot attend both; we cannot feast with God and feast with sin at the same time. This is God's invitation to us:

Come, all you who are thirsty, come to the waters;
and you who have no money, come, buy and eat!
Come, buy wine and milk without money and without cost.
Why spend money on what is not bread, and your labor on what does not satisfy?
Listen, listen to me, and eat what is good, and you will delight in the richest of fare. —Isaiah 55:1–2 (NIV)

Sin promises much, but it doesn't satisfy; it charges a high price. That price is broken lives, broken relationships, broken hopes. Ultimately the wages of sin is death. God offers us a feast that satisfies. He offers us delight for our souls. The motivation for change and holiness is this: God's feast is so much better! The price tag reads "No cost." There's no charge. It's His gift. Whose feast are you going to attend today? How can you strengthen your resolve?[4]

Nurture [10 minutes]

Imagine two homes side by side. In one God is hosting His feast. In the other sin is hosting its feast. Compare the two feasts.

What satisfaction do they offer? How lasting and real is that satisfaction? What price must you pay?

Do you suspect you don't really want to change? If so, what do you think might increase your desire?

Act [15 minutes]

Let's meditate on what it means to be a child of the Father.

Compare slavery to sin to being a child in God's family.

On the cross Jesus cried out, "It is finished." Imagine yourself answering back, "Not quite—there are still some things I need to do to finish the job." Think about how ridiculous and insulting this is.

Write a summary of why you would like to change, putting it in your own words in a way that resonates for you. Add some ideas of how you could strengthen your desire to change.

Later This Week [5 minutes]

Make plans to do something together this week just to be family together. Maybe you help do yard work at one of your homes and share lunch afterward. Maybe get all of your families together for dinner one night, go for a hike, play a game, or visit a museum. Maybe just go grocery shopping together.

Wrap it Up [5 minutes]

Briefly review what you learned today. Jot down the big-picture ideas in your own words. Discuss any final questions. Pray together.

This Week's Scripture Reading

As you read, ask the four questions slowly and prayerfully and remember the context. This is a letter from Paul writing to a church and believers like us to remind them of the who God is, what He has done, who we are, and how we live.

- Day 1: Ephesians 6:9
- Day 2: Ephesians 6:10–12
- Day 3: Ephesians 6:13–14
- Day 4: Ephesians 6:15–16
- Day 5: Ephesians 6:17–20
- Day 6: Ephesians 6:21–24

Notes:

WEEK 8

Rules

Week 8

Big Picture

- The law cannot restore our hearts
- The law points us to Jesus
- The gospel of Jesus is the power and means of our transformation

Opening [10 minutes]

Take a few minutes to see how each of you is doing and encourage each other. Be careful, as this time can easily get away from you. Make sure you talk about the "later this week" from the last time you got together. What are ways you can be in each other's lives more often than once a week?

Setup [1 minute]

Have you despaired of ever changing? Do you think you are a lost cause? Maybe you think it is different for you. Other people can change, but your history or temptations or problems make it different for you. The glorious good news of Jesus is that you and I can change.

Part of the problem is we often try to change in the wrong way.[5]

Discover

Read [10 minutes]

You have died with Christ, and He has set you free from the spiritual powers of this world. So why do you keep on following the rules of the world, such as, "Don't handle! Don't taste! Don't touch!"? Such rules are mere human teachings about things that deteriorate as we use them. These rules may seem wise because they require strong devotion, pious self-denial, and severe bodily discipline, but they provide no help in conquering a person's evil desires. —Colossians 2:20–23 (NLT)

Why do lists of religious rules often have an appearance of wisdom to us?

Do rules really provide no power in changing us? Why do you think that might be?

Article: How Are You Going to Change? [10 minutes]

It seems our first instinct when we want to change is to do something. We think activity will change us. We want a list of dos and don'ts. In Jesus's day people thought they could be pure through ceremonial washing. Today it can be spiritual disciplines or a set of laws. Many of these things are good in themselves, but they cannot change us inside.

"Are you so dull?" [Jesus] asked. "Don't you see that nothing that enters a person from the outside can defile them? For it doesn't go into their heart but into their stomach, and then out of the body." (In saying this, Jesus declared all foods clean.)

He went on: "What comes out of person is what defiles them. For it is from within, out of a person's heart, that evil thoughts come - sexual immorality, theft, murder, adultery, greed, malice, deceit, lewdness, envy, slander, arrogance, and folly. All these evils come from inside and defile a person." —Mark 7:18-23 (NIV)

External activities cannot change us, says Jesus, because sin comes from within, from our hearts. Our rituals might change our behavior for a while, but they cannot change our hearts. Therefore they cannot bring true and lasting holiness. We need heart change.[6]

What Law Can and Cannot Do

According to John Piper, there are at least three reasons why trying to "do" things or keep the law won't help us be transformed into Christ's image:

1. The Law Cannot Remove Our Condemnation.

The whole basis for transformation is the removal of condemnation; the law cannot remove it, and so the law cannot provide the basis for our transformation. If we want to be changed into the image of Jesus, we must first have the verdict of guilty reversed, and the law cannot do that—only God can because of Christ. We receive it by faith alone.

2. The Law Cannot Conquer the Flesh.

There is a second reason why the law cannot sanctify or transform: It cannot conquer the flesh. That is, it cannot change us at the root of our nature: our fallenness and rebellion against God. It cannot take away our reluctance to love God and our treasonous preference for God's gifts above God (Romans 1:23). On the contrary, Paul teaches us that the law aggravates our sin and stirs up our rebellion.

In other words the law is not the remedy for our condemnation or our rebellion. In fact, it is given to turn our inner rebellion into more blatant and visible transgressions. We see this again in Romans 7:5 (NASB), "While we were in the flesh, the sinful passions, which were aroused by the Law, were at work in the members of our body to bear fruit for death." In other words, the law does not conquer the flesh; it rouses the flesh. The law plays into the hands of our own sinful passions and stirs them up. We see the same thing in Romans 7:8 (NASB), "But sin, taking opportunity through the commandment, produced in me coveting of every kind." The law does not conquer the flesh; on the contrary, it gives the flesh another base of operation, another place to show its rebellion.

3. The Law Couldn't Give the Son the Glory for Justification and Sanctification.

The last reason the law cannot sanctify is seen at the end of Romans 5: God's purpose is to sanctify us in a way that the credit and the glory for our liberation and transformation go to Jesus Christ, not to ourselves and not to the law. Therefore God calls us not to turn to the law for transformation—for love and holiness and Christ-likeness—but to turn to the living Christ, who worked for us in history and works in us now by His Spirit.

The law cannot magnify the Son of God as more glorious and more valuable and more desirable than the pleasures of sin. Only when Christ Himself wins our affections over all contestants will He get the glory God means for Him to have. Even if you did turn to the law and experience some measure of success in becoming a law-abiding person (as the Pharisees certainly did, including Saul of Tarsus) Christ would get no honor from that. God's whole purpose in the plan of redemption is that His Son get the glory not only for our justification but also for our sanctification. This the law could not do.[7]

Trying to change through our own efforts to follow the rules (keep the law) is called legalism. We are all born legalists. We are convinced that our righteousness, our acceptability, is based on our performance, on what we know and what we do. The gospel says we have been forgiven by God and fully accepted by Him purely on the basis of what Jesus has done. If that's true, then any efforts of our own to add to the work of Jesus must be an offense to God! Isaiah 64:6 (NIV) says, "All our righteous acts are like filthy rags."

As Tim Keller likes to say, we need to repent of our damnable good works. Tim Keller expands on the nature of the gospel and the law:

"We never 'get beyond the gospel' in our Christian life to something more 'advanced.' The gospel is not the first 'step' in a 'stairway' of truths, rather, it is more like the 'hub' in a 'wheel' of truth. The gospel is not jut the A-B-C's of Christianity, but it is the A to Z of Christianity. We are not justified by the gospel and then sanctified by obedience but the gospel is the way we grow (Galatians 3:1-3) and are renewed (Colossians 1:6). It is the solution to each problem, the key to each closed door, the power through every barrier (Ro-

mans 1:16–17).

"All our problems come from a failure to apply the gospel. . . . The main problem, then, in the Christian life is that we have not thought out the deep implications of the gospel, we have not 'used' the gospel in and on all parts of our life. . . . The key to continual and deeper spiritual renewal and revival is the continual re-discovery of the gospel."

Nurture [20 minutes]

What are some things you've tried to do to change?

Why do you think those things are ultimately ineffective for bringing about lasting change? What are some areas where legalistic thinking present in your life?

What would it sound like to repent of your damnable good works?

How is Keller's explanation of the gospel related to our definition of discipleship?

Act [10 minutes]

Take some additional time to meditate on Keller's words. Then write out some implications of the gospel for your gospel change project. We'll be looking more at how we change next week.

Later This Week [1 minute]

Continue to think about the implications of the gospel on your gospel change project. Write down at least five.

Put in place whatever reminders you need to do this. How might you be able to hold each other accountable?

Wrap it Up [5 minutes]

Briefly review what you learned today. Jot down the big-picture ideas in your own words. Discuss any final questions. Pray together.

This Week's Scripture Reading

This week, we're shifting toward the Psalms to discover who God is, what He has done, who we are, and how we live. As you read these poems and songs, look for the truths about God that change who you are and how you live.

- Day 1: Psalm 43
- Day 2: Psalm 46
- Day 3: Psalm 47
- Day 4: Psalm 48
- Day 5: Psalm 50
- Day 6: Psalm 52

Notes:

WEEK 9

Freedom

Week 9

Leader's Note

Remind your DNA partners they are learning not just for themselves but in such a way as to be able to teach others to apply the gospel to every part of life.

Big Picture

- Change is God's work, but we have a role to play
- God the Father renews, liberates, and sanctifies us by His Spirit through Jesus
- We are both justified and sanctified by faith in the gospel

Opening [15 minutes]

Take a few minutes to see how each of you is doing and encourage each other. Be careful, as this time can easily get away from you.

Make sure you talk about the "later this week" from the last time you got together. Share a few of the five gospel's implications you wrote down for your change project. How is the process of this guide impacting the way you relate and engage others? Family? Community? Co-workers? Mission?

Setup [1 minute]

We saw last week that the law, although it has the appearance of wisdom, cannot restore our hearts. How can we grow and change? Is it up to us?

Discover

Read [15 minutes]

So then, my beloved, just as you have always obeyed, not as in my presence only, but now much more in my absence, work out your salvation with fear and trembling; for it is God who is at work in you, both to will and to work for His good pleasure. —Philippians 2:12–13 (NASB)

What do you think Paul means when he says to "work out your salvation with fear and trembling"?

> **Leader's Note**
>
> A few verses before, Paul reminded them that one day every knee would bow and tongue confess that Jesus Christ is Lord. "Working out our salvation" means to live out the implications of the gospel, especially in light of the fact that one day we will face Jesus as Lord and Savior (not Lord and Judge). We should want to obey Him in response to what He's done for us, and we should take that very seriously in light of His second coming.

Specifically, how is God at work in us? How does this connect to what we talked about last week?

Article: Change is God's Work [10 minutes]

Realizing that change is something that has to take place in the heart is just the first step in the battle for change. Once we understand this, it moves the battle for change from trying to modify our behaviors to trying to transform the deepest motivations of our hearts. However, this actually makes change harder, doesn't it? It is relatively easy to adjust our outward behavior for a little while, but this adjustment will never change who we are internally. In fact, the same old patterns of behavior always seem to pop up again and again because our hearts remain unchanged. We still naturally desire to seek our righteousness and our identity in things other than God Himself. The problem really is that we can't seem to change our own hearts!

We are not the first people to have experienced this problem. If we think back in God's Story to Deuteronomy we find Moses restating the Law that Israel was to keep because they had entered into a covenant relationship with God at Mt. Sinai. In the midst of urging Israel to "fear the Lord your God, to walk in all his ways, to love him, to serve the Lord your God with all your heart and with all your soul, and to keep the commandments and statues of the Lord, which I am commanding you today for your good" (Deut 10:12–13 ESV), he tells Israel in Deuteronomy 10:16 (ESV) to "circumcise therefore the foreskin of your heart, and be no longer stubborn." Circumcision was the outward sign that Israel was called by God to reflect His image to the world. However, Moses tells Israel that outward circumcision is not enough. Rather their hearts needed to be circumcised if they were going to be faithful to God.

The amazing thing is that later in Deuteronomy, Moses later tells Israel they would fall into unfaithfulness; rather than leaving them in their failure, God Himself would come and circumcise their hearts so they could live faithfully as God's people. This promise of God was echoed later in the Old Testament in places such as Ezekiel 36:

> *I will sprinkle clean water on you,*
> *and you will be clean;*
> *I will cleanse you from all your impurities*
> *and from all your idols. I will give you a new heart and put a new spirit in you;*
> *I will remove from you your heart of stone*
> *and give you a heart of flesh.*
> *And I will put my Spirit in you*
> *and move you to follow my decrees*
> *and be careful to keep my laws. —Ezekiel 36:25–27 (NIV)*

So change—both in our hearts and the actions that flow from our hearts—must come from God Himself! The Apostle Paul describes this amazing transformation in his letter to the Ephesians.

> *Blessed be the God and Father of our Lord Jesus Christ, who has blessed us in Christ with every spiritual blessing in the heavenly places, even as he chose us in him before the foundation of the world, that we should be holy and blameless before him. In love he predestined us for adoption as sons through Jesus Christ, according to the purpose of his will, to the praise of his glorious grace, with which he has blessed us in the Beloved. In him we have redemption through his blood, the forgiveness of our trespasses, according to the riches of his grace, which he lavished upon us, in all wisdom and insight making known to us the mystery of his will, according to his purpose, which he set forth in Christ as a plan for the fullness of time, to unite all things in him, things in heaven and things on earth. In him we have obtained an inheritance, having been predestined according to the purpose of him who works all things according to the counsel of his will, so that we who were the first to hope in Christ might be to the praise of his glory. In him you also, when you heard the word of truth, the gospel of your salvation, and believed in him, were sealed with the promised Holy Spirit, who is the guarantee of our inheritance until we acquire possession of it, to the praise of his glory. —Ephesians 1:3–14 (ESV)*

Notice here how the full power and energy of God are at work to liberate us from our oppressive sinful nature and desires! The Father desired to set us free from the sinful desires that enslave us and restore our status as sons and daughters. He set in motion a plan carried out by His Son Jesus and the Spirit to deliver us from both the penalty and power of sin.

Jesus does what legalism can never do: He gives us a new heart and a new spirit. Without that inner transformation we can never please God. People are not changed by therapy or analysis—not even biblical analysis. They are changed by God (You Can Change, p. 53). The Father renews, liberates, and sanctifies through the Son by the Spirit.

Sanctified by Faith in the Gospel

Even though Jesus reconciles us to the Father through the Spirit entirely by His work, this doesn't mean we get to put our feet up and relax as though we had nothing to do. Even though the Spirit's power accomplishes both our reconciliation to the Father and our transformation into the Son's image, every day we are faced with the choice to submit to His leadership or to go our own way. We must enter into a process of daily repentance and faith in the truth of the gospel as we choose to entrust ourselves entirely to God. Understanding what Jesus has done for us and worshipping God in response is the only thing that will bring lasting change.

Tim Keller describes it this way:

> *Paul says to Christians, 'your life is hid with Christ in God' (Col 3:3), and in numerous places he says that we are now 'in him.' This means, on the one hand, that the Father accepts us in Christ and treats us as if we had done all that Jesus has done (cf. Col 3:2a). But this is also means Christ's life comes into us by the Spirit and shapes us into a new kind of person. The gospel is not just a truth about us that we affirm with our minds, it is also a reality we must experience in our hearts and souls. For example, In 2 Corinthians 8 and 9 Paul wants the people to give an offering to the poor. He says, "I don't want to order you. I don't want this offering to simply be the response to my demand." He doesn't put pressure directly on the will (saying 'I'm an apostle and this is your duty to me!') nor pressure directly on the emotions (telling them stories about how much the poor are suffering and how much more they have than the sufferers). Instead, Paul vividly and unforgettably says, "You know the grace of our Lord Jesus Christ, that though he was rich, yet for your sakes he became poor, so that you through his poverty might become rich" (2 Cor 8:9). When he says 'you know the grace'—he uses a powerful image, bringing Jesus' salvation into the realm of money and wealth and poverty. He moves them by a 'spiritual recollection' of the gospel. Paul is saying, 'Think on his costly grace. Think on that grace until you are changed into generous people by the gospel in your hearts.' So the solution to stinginess is a re-orientation to the*

generosity of Christ in the gospel, where he poured out his wealth for you. Now you don't have to worry about money—the cross proves God's care for you and gives you security. Now you don't have to envy any one else's money. Jesus' love and salvation confers on you a remarkable status—one that money cannot give you.

Paul does the same thing in Ephesians 5:25ff, where he urges husbands to be faithful to their wives. What is the point? What makes you a sexually faithful spouse, a generous person, or a good parent is not just redoubled effort to follow the example of Christ. Rather, it is deepening your understanding of the salvation of Christ and living out of the changes that understanding makes in your heart—the seat of your mind, will, and emotions. Faith in the gospel re-structures our motivations, our self-understanding and identity, and our view of the world. Behavioral compliance to rules without heart-change will be superficial and fleeting. The gospel changes your heart.[8]

Nurture [20 minutes]

How is God at work in you? What evidences have you seen that God is transforming you throughout the last year or two?

What evidence is there that He has changed (circumcised) your heart and given you a new heart?

What is our role in being conformed to the image of Jesus?

Act [10 minutes]

Write a summary of how you are praying God will change you and a summary of how God has changed you.[13]

Write down the aspect of God's work of change that especially gives you confidence that you can change. [9]

Later This Week

Read what you wrote in the exercise above at least three times (or even every day) this week. Put in place whatever reminders you need to do this. How might you be able to hold each other accountable?

Wrap it Up [5 minutes]

Briefly review what you learned today. Jot down the big-picture ideas in your own words. Discuss any final questions. Pray together.

This Week's Scripture Reading

We're continuing in the Psalms to discover who God is, what He has done, who we are, and how we live. As you read these poems and songs look for the truths about God that change who you are and how you live.

- Day 1: Psalm 54
- Day 2: Psalm 55
- Day 3: Psalm 56
- Day 4: Psalm 57
- Day 5: Psalm 65
- Day 6: Psalm 67

Notes:

WEEK 10

Worship

Week 10

Big Picture

- God uses everything that happens to us—even our struggles—to make us more like Jesus
- My behavior comes from my heart
- My circumstances trigger my heart
- We sin because we do not trust God and do not worship God

Opening [10 minutes]

Take a few minutes to see how each of you is doing and encourage each other. Be careful, as this time can easily get away from you. Make sure you talk about the "later this week" from the last time you got together.

Setup [1 minute]

Our struggles reveal our hearts. Why do we do the things we do? Where do evil thoughts, sexual immorality, theft, murder, adultery, greed, and malice all come from? Jesus gives us the answer. . . .

Discover

Read [10 minutes]

Don't you see that nothing that enters a person from the outside can defile them? For it doesn't go into their heart but into their stomach, and then out of the body... For it is from within, out of a person's heart, that evil thoughts come—sexual immorality, theft, murder, adultery, greed, malice, deceit, lewdness, envy, slander, arrogance and folly. All these evils come from inside and defile a person. —Mark 7:18–19, 21-23 (NIV)

For whatever does not proceed from faith is sin. —Romans 14:23 (ESV)

Pray Together [10 minutes]

Pray together through these passages. You may talk with the Father about questions such as this:

What kinds of things have you seen come out of your heart? Pray for each other. Ask God to give you the wisdom and grace to live by faith.

Article: All of Life is Worship [10 minutes]

From the Story we can see that humans were made to worship. We were made to adore, to long for, to delight in, to desire. We were made to have the deepest longings of our hearts met by someone or something outside of ourselves.

When we look to something for significance, acceptance, approval, satisfaction, fulfillment, joy, security, etc., that very act is worship. We are ascribing worth to something. We are saying, "That thing is what will make me significant! That person will make me acceptable. That person will give me security. That thing will save me!"

You see, all of life is worship. We are ALWAYS worshiping. Everything we do is an affirmation of who or what we are looking to for significance, security, approval, etc.

Your life is a billboard; you are advertising the thing that is most important to you. "This is what I value! This is what saves me!" That constant advertisement, "Here's what I'm all about!" is worship. All of life is worship.

Your life is a garden hose that is always on. Worship always flows out of us like water out of that hose. Where are we going to point the hose? Something is going to get wet with our worship. Who or what is it?

There is no neutral on the worship gearshift of your life. You are always in gear, and you are always in drive or reverse. Romans 1:25 (ESV) says we've "exchanged the truth about God for a lie and worshiped and served the creature rather than the Creator."

Every sin is a finger-wagging accusation against God! Every time we sin, we are saying to God, "You are not great! You are not in control! You are not good! THIS THING OVER HERE WILL SAVE ME!" Do you hear how offensive that is!?

We all worship false gods. We all look to created things instead of the Creator for acceptance, approval, satisfaction, etc. This false worship produces all kinds of negative behaviors and emotions in our lives, which we call sin. These sin issues are not merely behavior problems. They are heart issues.

What comes out of a person is what defiles him. For from within, out of the heart of man, come evil thoughts, sexual immorality, theft, murder, adultery, coveting, wickedness, deceit, sensuality, envy, slander, pride, foolishness. All these evil things come from within, and they defile a person. —Mark 7:20–23 (ESV)

According to the Bible, the heart is far more than a muscle in your chest pumping blood throughout your body.

The word "heart" occurs more 850 times in the Bible. If you looked up all of those uses of the word, you'd find that our heart makes decisions, it feels emotion, can be deceived, desires things, lusts, thinks, and reasons.

The word "heart" is the word the Bible uses to describe the real you, the very center of your being. The heart includes your mind, your will, and your emotions. It is not less than any one of those things; it is more.

Above all else, guard your heart, for it is the wellspring of life. —Proverbs 4:23 (NIV)

A wellspring is a naturally occurring water source that continually produces. The water continues to flow outward from the source. If you want to know whether or not the fruit of the source is suitable for drinking, you've got to go to the source and sample the water.

Our hearts are like a wellspring, continually producing fruit. Everything in our lives flows outward from this source we call our hearts. The fruit of our lives is an indicator of the state of our hearts. Our behavior comes from our hearts.

How would most people you know answer the question, "What needs to change?"

They might say:

- Their circumstances (better job, lose weight, get married)
- Their behavior (I just need to be more patient, I need to worry less)
- Their self-concept (I just need to believe in myself or have more self-confidence)

But what really needs to change? Their heart!

What causes fights and quarrels among you? Don't they come from your desires that battle within you? You desire but do not have, so you kill. You covet but you cannot get what you want, so you quarrel and fight. You do not have because you do not ask God. When you ask, you do not receive, because you ask with wrong motives, that you may spend what you get on your pleasures.
—James 4:1–3 (NIV)

Typically people want to blame their sin on their circumstances. I got angry because the guy cut me off in traffic. I started to worry all of the time because my husband lost his job. I yelled at the kids because they weren't obeying me.

But the reality is that our circumstances merely reveal what is already in our hearts!

Our struggles reveal our hearts. That means they are a great opportunity to tackle the heart causes of our sinful behavior and negative emotions.

So what is it that is going on in our hearts? The Bible says two things are happening in our hearts. Hebrews 4:12 (NET) speaks of "the desires and thoughts of the heart":

- we think, interpret, make sense, trust
- we desire, worship, want, treasure[10]

Human beings are always interpreting or making sense of our environment and our circumstances. Humans are always worshipping. We were created to worship. It's what we're designed to do, and our worship never stops.

So there are two potential ways sin can take root in our hearts: We can think or believe wrong things about God, or we can worship and desire wrong things other than God. Sin happens when we believe lies about God instead of God's Word and when we worship idols instead of worshipping God.[11] When it comes to sinful patterns in our lives, efforts to modify our behavior will never be effective. We worshipped our way into the problem, and we will worship our way out.

Destructive or sinful behaviors such as lying, manipulation, violence, theft, adultery, addictions, and eating disorders, and negative or sinful emotions such as anxiety, depression, envy, guilt, bitterness, and pride all arise when our hearts do not trust God and do not worship God. The solution is faith and repentance. The gospel invites us to faith and repentance. The key is to make the link between our specific sins and the lies and idols in our hearts.[12]

Trust God instead of believing lies = faith

Worship God instead of worshiping idols = repentance

Nuture

"There is no neutral on the worship gear shift of your life. You are always in gear, and you are always in drive or reverse." What gear is the "worship" gear shift of your life in most of the time? Drive or reverse?

Why does the writer of Proverbs encourage us to "above all else, guard your heart"? What's so key about the heart? What do your struggles reveal about your heart? Answer this question specifically, not generically. These additional questions may help:

- What did you want, desire, or wish for?
- What did you fear? What were you worrying about?
- What did you think you needed?
- What were your strategies and intentions designed to accomplish?
- What or whom were you trusting?
- Whom were you trying to please? Whose opinion of you counted?
- What were you loving? What were you hating?
- What would have you brought you the greatest happiness, pleasure, or delight?
- What would have brought you the greatest pain and misery?
- Think about the issue you're addressing with your gospel change project.
- When are you typically tempted in this area?
- What hard circumstances seem to trigger this temptation?

Act [10 minutes]

Begin writing a summary of when you sin and what is going on in your heart. We'll be thinking more about what's going on in our hearts in the next few weeks.

Later This Week [1 minute]

Complete your summary from the "nurture" section during the week. Take some time to ponder the questions prayerfully.

What do your struggles reveal about your heart?

Put in place whatever reminders you need to do this. How might you be able to hold each other accountable?

Leader's Note

Next week's article is long and thorough. You will want everyone to read that article thoughtfully before you get together so you will have time to discuss. Encourage folks to highlight sentences that stick out to them and write questions they have.

Wrap it Up [5 minutes]

Briefly review what you learned today. Jot down the big-picture ideas in your own words. Discuss any final questions. Pray together.

This Week's Scripture Reading

This is our last week in the Psalms. These Psalms focus on worship. As you read continue to ask the four questions. These Psalms are about God and our posture toward Him. As you walk through the final questions, consider your heart and posture toward God. What do you believe about God and what He has done? What does your life reveal about what you worship and believe about God?

- Day 1: Psalm 95
- Day 2: Psalm 96
- Day 3: Psalm 97
- Day 4: Psalm 98
- Day 5: Psalm 99
- Day 6: Psalm 100

Notes:

WEEK 11

Truth

Week 11

Big Picture

This is where we're going—the big ideas to understand more deeply this week.

- The truth shall set you free
- All sin comes from lies we believe about God
- God is great, so I don't have to be in control
- God is glorious, so we do not have to fear others
- God is good, so we do not have to look elsewhere
- God is gracious, so we do not have to prove ourselves

Opening [10 minutes]

Take a few minutes to see how each of you is doing and encourage each other. Be careful, this time can easily get away from you. Make sure you talk about the "later this week" from the last time you got together. Read each other the summaries you wrote about what is going on in your hearts when you sin.

Setup [1 minute]

Behind every sin and negative emotion is a lie. Every time we don't trust God or His word then we are believing something else: a lie. Life and freedom are found by trusting and delighting in the truth about God. Our problems are created by the gaps between what we believe in theory and what we believe in practice. We need to learn to preach the truth about God to our hearts.

Pray Together [10 minutes]

Pray together and ask the Father to set you free from lies and to give you the grace to cling to Jesus as the truth.

Discover

Read [15 minutes]

Now the serpent was more crafty than any other beast of the field that the Lord God had made.

He said to the woman, "Did God actually say, 'You shall not eat of any tree in the garden'?" And the woman said to the serpent, "We may eat of the fruit of the trees in the garden, but God said, 'You shall not eat of the fruit of the tree that is in the midst of the garden, neither shall you touch it, lest you die.'" But the serpent said to the woman, "You will not surely die. For God knows that when you eat of it your eyes will be opened, and you will be like God, knowing good and evil." So when the woman saw that the tree was good for food, and that it was a delight to the eyes, and that the tree was to be desired to make one wise, she took of its fruit and ate, and she also gave some to her husband who was with her, and he ate. Then the eyes of both were opened, and they knew that they were naked. And they sewed fig leaves together and made themselves loincloths.

And they heard the sound of the Lord God walking in the garden in the cool of the day, and the man and his wife hid themselves from the presence of the Lord God among the trees of the garden. But the Lord God called to the man and said to him, "Where are you?" And he said, "I heard the sound of you in the garden, and I was afraid, because I was naked, and I hid myself." He said, "Who told you that you were naked? Have you eaten of the tree of which I commanded you not to eat?" The man said, "The woman whom you gave to be with me, she gave me fruit of the tree, and I ate." Then the Lord God said to the woman, "What is this that you have done?" The woman said, "The serpent deceived me, and I ate." —Genesis 3:1–13 (ESV)

What did Adam and Eve choose to do in this story?

> **Leader's Note**
>
> You may need to lead the discussion beyond "ate the fruit" deeper toward answers such as: Believe the lie of the serpent, choose NOT to trust God's words, trust in self apart from God, trust in their own abilities to manage good and evil in their lives.

What was the real temptation the serpent presented to Adam and Eve?

What do you think was going on in their hearts?

> **Leader's Note**
>
> › Everyone should read this article individually.

Article: What Truths Do You Need to Turn To? [10 minutes]

The root of all our behavior and emotions is the heart: what it trusts and what it treasures. We sin because we believe the lie that we should be God: that His rule is oppressive, that we will be free without Him, that living for self offers more than what God provides. We might never be so bold as to voice this kind of thinking, but this unbelief is at the root of every sin and every negative emotion.

Therefore, the problem is that we are all unbelievers—all of us! Not many Christians think of themselves as unbelievers! After all we normally use the term to describe people who are not yet disciples of Jesus at all. There are many things about God we actually do not believe. Often there is a large difference, or a large gap, between what we know in our head and what we truly believe in our heart.

It is what we truly believe in the core of our being, in our heart, that affects our actions. The heart is "the wellspring of life" and "with the heart a person believes" (Romans 10:10 NASB).

We may know (and even say we believe) that God is in control of all things, that He is sovereign . . .but then we are filled with worry and anxiety about many of the details of our lives! It's as if we are saying, "I know God is in control, but I don't really believe God is in control. Therefore I must work to control certain parts of my life."

The process of closing the gap between what we know in our head and what we believe in our heart is called sanctification. Sanctification is about becoming more like Jesus, but we will only become more like Jesus when our actions are consistent with what we say we believe.

The Truth Shall Set You Free

Last week we talked about believing the truth about God (faith) and desiring God above all other things (worship).

When we ask what truths you need to turn to, we're not talking about knowing the right mantra about God to chant when you are faced with temptation. Saying "God is in control" over and over and over again will usually not stem the tide of worry and anxiety in our hearts. We must exercise faith in the greatness of God, and we must worship Him as the Great One to win the battle against sin.

Imagine you have never tasted honey. You might possess the knowledge of its sweetness because people you trust have told you it is sweet, but that is very different from possessing a belief in its sweetness that can only come from the mouth-watering experience of honey on your tongue.[14] When we truly believe God and experience the reality of who He is (by tasting and seeing

He is good), our desire for God will grow exponentially.

Whether we've already sinned or we're being tempted to sin, we need to speak truth to ourselves and worship God by telling Him the truth about Himself. You cannot worship God and sin at the same time.

We will summarize four life-changing truths about God:[15]

1. God is great, so we do not have to be in control.
2. God is glorious, so we do not have to fear others.
3. God is good, so we do not have to look elsewhere.
4. God is gracious, so we do not have to prove ourselves.

For many, these four truths have become an extremely helpful tool that allows us see our sin at a heart-level.

1. God is great, so we do not have to be in control.

Great is the LORD and most worthy of praise; his greatness no one can fathom. —Psalm 145:3 (NIV)

A fathom is a unit of measurement used to determine the depth of large bodies of water. When David says no one can fathom God's greatness, he's not just saying we can't understand it. He's saying if we had a fathom-stick and tried to measure the greatness of God, we would not be able to do it!

God is great. He has all power. There is nothing He cannot do. He is in control of the entire universe. A word we sometimes use to describe the greatness of God is sovereignty.

"God is sovereign" means He is in control of all things, that nothing escapes His notice, that nothing happens He doesn't know about, that HE is the one who keeps the earth spinning on its axis and rotating around the sun. God is great!

Our knowledge of God's greatness seems to go out the window as soon as things don't go our way. We get stuck in traffic. Our kids don't obey. There's too much month left at the end of the paycheck. How do we respond? By trying to be in control! We see this in nearly every area of our lives: time, career, money, relationships, other people's actions, people's impressions of us.

What do these efforts to control produce in us? Worry, busyness, frustration, stress, controlling or manipulating others, lack of gentleness, pride (when things go well), guilt (when things do not go well).

Nowhere in God's Story is His power more clearly on display than in the story of Jesus.

He was born of a virgin. He lived a perfect sinless life, submitted fully to the Father, something no human had ever done. On the cross the countless sins of billions of humans were piled on Him, and His death was sufficient to pay the penalty for all of them. Jesus overcame death by raising from the dead, undoing the curse of sin that had reigned since the garden of Eden. He sent His Spirit to live inside of humans, empowering them to do the same works He accomplished on earth.

For Jews demand miraculous signs and Greeks ask for wisdom, but we preach about a crucified Christ, a stumbling block to Jews and foolishness to Gentiles. But to those who are called, both Jews and Greeks, Christ is the power of God and the wisdom of God. —1 Corinthians 1:22–24 (NET)

Jesus is the wisdom and the power of God! Repent of your desire to be in control. Believe that God, through His Son Jesus, has clearly demonstrated His greatness. Worship Him as the One True Sovereign. The truth will set you free.

2. God is glorious, so we do not have to fear others.

One common reason we sin is that we crave the approval of other people or we fear their rejection and disapproval. We "need" the acceptance of others, so we are controlled by them. The Bible's term for this is "fear of man." "Fear of man will prove to be a snare, but whoever trusts in the Lord is kept safe" (Proverbs 29:25 NIV). Ed Welch in his book *When People are Big and God is Small*[16] says fear of man has many symptoms: susceptibility to peer pressure; "needing" something from a spouse; a concern with self-esteem; being over-committed because we can't say no; fear of being exposed; small lies to make yourself look good; people making you jealous, angry, depressed or anxious; avoiding people; comparing yourself to others; and fear of talking about Jesus.[17]

Our culture tries to overcome this problem by finding ways to bolster self-esteem, but this actually compounds the problem. We become dependent on whatever or whoever will boost our self-esteem. In reality low self-esteem is thwarted pride—we do not have the status we think we deserve.

We use the language of "need." We elevate often-good desires (love, affirmation, respect) to needs without which we think we cannot be whole. We talk about "needing" the approval or acceptance of other people, but our true need is to glorify God and love other people.

The answer to fear of man is fear of God. We need a big view of God. "*He will be the sure foundation for your times,*" says Isaiah, "*a rich store of salvation and wisdom and knowledge; the fear of the Lord is the key to this treasure*" (Isaiah 33:6 NIV). The key to God's treasure is to fear Him. To fear God is to respect, worship, trust, and submit to God. It is the proper response to His glory, holiness, power, love, goodness, and wrath.

Jesus is the glory of the Father. "Glory" means "weight," as in "a person of importance, a weighty person." Jesus shows us the full weight, the full significance of the character and nature of God. Jesus shows us God as He really is. God, in all of His majesty, splendor, wisdom, beauty, power, compassion, grace, patience, and love, was put on display in the person of Jesus Christ.

Now imagine Jesus the glorious One and the person you fear standing side by side. Who is the most glorious, beautiful, holy, awesome, and majestic? [18]

3. God is good, so we do not have to look elsewhere.

From the very beginning, God created humans with needs. They needed food, water, rest, work to accomplish, relationship, and intimacy. God would meet these needs abundantly. Because God is good, He gives us good things to satisfy these basic needs. God doesn't exist for us; we exist for Him, to live in dependent and submitted relationship with Him. This pattern of our need and His provision (over and over and over again every single day) show us this.

These things all point to deeper spiritual realities in our lives, too. Every physical need you have is a picture of your spiritual need! Your body needs rest, and your soul needs rest. Your body is thirsty, and your soul is thirsty. Your body is hungry, and your soul is hungry. Your body needs love and intimacy, and your soul needs love and intimacy. God in His goodness meets the needs of your body, and God in His goodness is the only one who can meet the needs of your soul!

There is a pattern: God creates the need, and He fills it. God is the source of all life and the giver of all good gifts (James 1:17). God meets our physical needs with good things, and He meets our deeper needs with the ultimate good thing: Himself.

Yet we often look to the created gifts for satisfaction and fulfillment instead of looking to the One who gives the gifts. We want God's provision, but we don't want God.

What do you look to for satisfaction? What are you saying when you say, "When I have THIS, then everything will be okay"?

Knowing our tendency to look to created things instead of the Creator, Jesus came, saying, "I am the bread of life. Whoever comes to me will never go hungry" (John 6:35 NIV). He said, "Whoever drinks the water I give them will never thirst" (John 4:14 NIV). He's not talking about cannibalism as the way to fill your hungry stomach forever or some magic water that will quench your thirst forever. He's talking about feeding on Him in a spiritual sense, having your hungry and thirsty soul filled by the very giver of life itself. "Taste and see that the Lord is good" (Psalm 34:8 NIV).

It is easy to think that following Jesus is somehow a lesser existence, that living for our own pleasures and pursuing fulfillment through every created is somehow the "good life." But a life lived in obedience to the Father through His Spirit is the true good life! Obedience is a blessing, and God has given us Himself so we don't have to look elsewhere.

4. God is gracious, so we do not have to prove ourselves.

Christians love to talk about the grace of God. We often say, "I know God is gracious. He forgave my sins so I will not go to hell when I die." Still we work really hard to prove ourselves. When it comes to grace, there is a large gap between what we know and what we believe.

What does it mean when we say that God is gracious? Webster's defines grace as "the freely given, unmerited favor and love of God." Grace is unmerited favor; undeserved favor; being given something that you did not deserve.

God *is* gracious. Because of our sin, the only thing we deserve from God is death. Through the life, death, burial, and resurrection of Jesus, He offers us life. The only thing we have to do to receive God's grace is accept it. When we do, we are made right with Him. We are fully accepted and loved by God. There's nothing we have done to earn it, and there's nothing we can do to lose it. There's nothing left to prove.

Much of the time, we live as though we do deserve things, that we've proven something to someone. We live with a sense of entitlement. We feel as though our own hard work and performance has merited us something, either from God or from other people. This is the same as looking God in the eye and saying, "You are not gracious. All I have is not a free gift from you. I've worked hard to earn it. I have proven myself to you, and now you are obligated to bless me."

This heart posture manifests itself through pride, self-righteousness toward people who are not as "good," extreme guilt when we fail to perform, and anger when we don't get what we feel we deserve. Fundamentally what we are saying is that we are not defined by the work of Jesus on our behalf, but rather we are defined by our own work.

Jesus lived the life we could never live and died the death we should have died. When we place our faith and trust in Him, we are freed from pride and guilt. We know our efforts to prove ourselves did not make us right with God (no pride), and we know when our efforts to prove ourselves come up short, we are forgiven (no guilt).

Pride and guilt are replaced with confidence and humility: confidence because the performance of Jesus makes me acceptable to God (in spite of my failures), and humility because I constantly need the grace of God (because of my ongoing failures). I do not have to prove myself.

We will be tempted over and over to stop believing that God is great, glorious, good, and gracious. When we face temptation we need to say not only I should not do this, but also I need not do this. When we're tempted to overeat, we shouldn't just say, "I should not be a glutton," but we can also say, "I need not overeat because God is good." When we're tempted to freak out about an uncertain situation, we shouldn't just say, "I should not be afraid," but we can also say, "I need not fear because God is great." Whatever sin offers, God is bigger and better. To say to temptation "I must not do this" is legalism. To say "I need not do this" is gospel. [19]

Nurture [20 minutes]

What is the difference between knowing something in your head and believing it in your heart? How do you know when there is gap between these two in your life?

What do you think it means to "know the truth" if knowing is more than acquiring information or agreeing to statements?

What do you think this sentence means: "You cannot worship God and sin at the same time"?

What areas of your life are you tempted to control? What is the lie you are believing when you seek to control those areas?

Who do you sometimes fear more than God?

Leader's Note

If answers don't come right away, suggest boss, parents, spouse, children, friends, etc.

What do you look to for satisfaction? What are you saying right now, "When I have THIS, then everything will be okay"? How does Jesus show the goodness of God?

What are some evidences in your behavior or emotions that you are trying to prove yourself?

What is the lie behind the area you have chosen in your gospel change project?

How does Jesus provide the greatness, glory, goodness, and grace your heart craves?

Act [15 minutes]

Write a summary of the truths you need to turn to in faith, particularly regarding your gospel change project.

Later This Week [1 minute]

Choose a part of the Story of God you think portrays well the truth about God you need to be reminded of. Come ready to share it next time. Also try to notice when your heart goes toward wanting to be in control this week.

Put in place whatever reminders you need to do this. How might you be able to hold each other accountable?

Wrap it Up [5 minutes]

Briefly review what you learned today. Jot down the big-picture ideas in your own words. Discuss any final questions. Pray together.

This Week's Scripture Reading

This is our last week in the Psalms. These Psalms focus on worship. As you read continue to ask the four questions. These Psalms are about God and our posture toward Him. As you walk through the final questions, consider your heart and posture toward God. What do you believe about God and what He has done? What does your life reveal about what you worship and believe about God?

- Day 1: Psalm 123
- Day 2: Psalm 124
- Day 3: Psalm 125
- Day 4: Psalm 128
- Day 5: Psalm 130
- Day 6: Psalm 135

Notes:

WEEK 12

Idolatry

Week 12

Big Picture

- Idolatry manifests itself in many different ways in our lives
- We desire or worship idols instead of worshipping God
- Idolatry is false worship
- God is jealous and pours out His wrath in response to idolatry

Opening [10 minutes]

Take a few minutes to see how each of you is doing and encourage each other. Be careful, as this time can easily get away from you. Make sure you talk about the "later this week" from the last time you got together. Share the truth about God most relevant to your gospel change project and the part of the Story that reveals it, inspiring worship.

Setup [1 minute]

We said to ourselves last week, "God is all I need." Influenced by lies about God instead of God's Word, our desires (they usually feel like needs) are often for things other than God and His glory.

Discover

Read [10 minutes]

Prepare your minds for action; be self-controlled; set your hope fully on the grace to be given you when Jesus Christ is revealed. As obedient children, do not conform to the evil desires you had when you lived in ignorance. But just as he who called you is holy, so be holy in all you do. —1 Peter 1:13–15 (NIV)

What do you think it means to "set your hope fully on the grace to be given you when Jesus is revealed"? What are some of the evil desires that still plague your life?

Article: What Idols Do You Need to Turn From?

[10 minutes]

For they exchanged the truth of God for a lie, and worshiped and served the creature rather than the Creator, who is blessed forever. Amen. —Romans 1:25 (NASB)

Often this verse can conjure up images of tribal people bowing down to a small piece of wood, carved to resemble a person or an animal, and offering bits of food to appease the false deity.

But "the exchange of truth for lie is the essence of idolatry, and idolatry, in turn, underlies all sin." [21]

Idolatry may sound primitive, but it is alive and well. It pervades not only our culture but our own lives. All of us worship and serve created things rather than the Creator.

Tim Keller defines an idol in several different ways:

- Anything more important to you than God
- Anything that absorbs your heart and imagination more than God
- Anything you seek to give you what only God can give
- Whatever you look at and say in your heart of hearts, "If I have that, then I'll feel my life has meaning, then I'll know I have value, then I'll feel significant and secure"
- Anything that becomes more fundamental than God to your happiness, meaning in life, and identity[22]
- On the surface, idolatry can manifest itself in many different ways:
  - Greed and materialism
  - Lust for achievement/success

- Approval of man/fear of man
- Codependent relationship with a child or spouse
- Porn/sexual addiction
- Desire for power and control
- Anger
- Addiction to drugs, alcohol, food, or entertainment

Idolatry sounds like this:

"I will give something up to have it. I will sacrifice to get it. I will compromise, and I will beg, borrow, or steal to possess it. I will lie, cheat, or steal. It is the chief pursuit of my life. I am restless until it is mine."

The manifestation of idolatry is merely an indicator of a deeper heart issue. Remember what we've said about worship: that we are created to worship, that we are always worshipping? Idolatry in our lives is merely another indicator of the worship direction of our hearts.

For example, people can idolize their spouse. They can connect all of their sense of security and significance and acceptance to what their spouse thinks of them. (This can be true for people who do not even have a spouse).

What is that person really saying about who God is?

What are they saying about the work of God?

Idolatry is always twin idolatry. It's never just about the false god. There's always a second idol involved.

If a mother sets her children up as an idol, she may pin all of her hope for significance on their performance. What she believes about herself—her worth and value—is completely based on how well she performs as a mother. If her kids behave and end up becoming successful adults, then she will feel smug and proud about all of her hard work as mom. If they misbehave and don't turn out so well, she will be embarrassed and feel like a failure. Her kids are the key to her happiness and sense of worth. They are her idol.

It takes an idol to make an idol. The day that mother set those children up as an idol, effectively saying, "They are god, and God is not," she was also saying, "I am god, and God is not." Who else but God can determine what is worthy of worship!

The number-one created thing I worship is the created thing I see looking back at me in the mirror every morning. Any establishment of an idol is an act of selfish rebellion and is essentially saying, "I am god. I am the most important being in the whole universe. I will pursue my own agenda, and I will call the shots. I am god. The Creator is not."

Shortly after God delivered his people from Egypt, He descended on Mt. Sinai in the form of a terrible storm and gave them the Ten Commandments.

I am the LORD your God, who brought you out of Egypt, out of the land of slavery. You shall have no other gods before me. You shall not make for yourself an image in the form of anything in heaven above or on the earth beneath or in the waters below. You shall not bow down to them or worship them; for I, the LORD your God, am a jealous God. —Exodus 20:2–5 (NIV)

The people responded by saying repeatedly, "Everything the Lord has said we will do!" (Exodus 19:8; 24:3, 7 NIV). A few weeks later, after Moses had spent nearly forty days on the mountain with God, the people asked Moses' brother Aaron to "make us gods who will go before us" (Exodus 32:1 NIV). They constructed a calf out of gold and bowed down to it, declaring it was the god who had brought them out of Egypt (Exodus 32:4). Their desire for a god they could see and their inability to trust the God who had saved them led them to worship an idol. They broke the second commandment because they had already broken the first. It takes an idol to make an idol. The stunning departure of God's people filled Him with righteous wrath. He basically told Moses to step back so He could wipe them all out and start over with Moses (Exodus 32:10).

Moses stepped forward. He interceded on behalf of the people, begging God to change His mind. God withheld judgment on the whole group. God still poured out His wrath; at least 3,000 people ended up dying, but the death of some saved the lives of the many.

Now imagine the Creator, our Father, and His grief over our idolatry. Every commandment we break is preceded by our breaking of the first commandment. It takes an idol to make an idol. God could rightly say of humanity, "I'm going to wipe them all out!" But Jesus steps forward and intercedes. God withholds His judgment on the whole group. God still pours out His wrath, and the death of one saves the lives of countless.

Jesus is our better Moses. He takes the wrath of God we deserve as idol worshippers, and He lives to make intercession for us continually as we mess up over and over again.

My little children, I am writing these things to you so that you may not sin And if anyone sins, we have an Advocate with the Father, Jesus Christ the righteous; and He Himself is the propitiation for our sins; and not for ours only, but also for those of the whole world. —1 John 2:1–2 (NASB)

To propitiate means to satisfy. God's righteous wrath against humanity has been satisfied through Jesus. He will still pour out His wrath on those who reject the sacrificial offering Jesus made, but Jesus' death was sufficient to satisfy all of God's wrath against sinful humans.

Nurture [15 minutes]

What are some of the evidences that you worship idols?

What are some of the idols you tend to worship?

Explain how idolizing someone or something is you setting yourself up as an idol. ("It takes an idol to make an idol.")

Just based on what you read today, how would you explain Jesus's intercession and propitiation?

Act [20 minutes]

You may want to review weeks eight through ten before completing this exercise. Begin the exercise together and finish it later this week.

Pray together and ask the Spirit to reveal some of the specific idols in your life.

What idol do you think is behind the issue you're addressing in your gospel change project? Write these out.

Then identify the lie or misplaced desire that is behind each idol. (Ask, "What am I saying about God when you worship that idol?")

Finally, write down the truth about God you need to believe when you are tempted to worship those idols.

Later This Week [1 minute]

Continue the exercise above, writing down your thoughts on each question. Check in with each other mid-week to see how this is going.

Put in place whatever reminders you need to do this. How might you be able to hold each other accountable?

Wrap it Up [5 minutes]

Briefly review what you learned today. Jot down the big-picture ideas in your own words. Discuss any final questions. Pray together.

This Week's Scripture Reading

We're now shifting toward narrative in the Gospel of Luke. As you read these stories look for the truths about God that change who you are and how you live. Who do we see Jesus to be in these stories, and what has He done through them? How does Jesus change who people are? What is He calling them to do?

- Day 1: Luke 5:1–26
- Day 2: Luke 7:11–17
- Day 3: Luke 7:36–50
- Day 4: Luke 8:22–56
- Day 5: Luke 14:25–33
- Day 6: Luke 17: 1–19

Notes:

WEEK 13

Repentance & Faith

Week 13

Big Picture

- Sin arises because we desire something more than we desire God
- Continual repentance
- We repent by faith
- God is bigger and better than my sinful desires

Opening [10 minutes]

Take a few minutes to see how each of you is doing and encourage each other. Be careful, as this time can easily get away from you. Make sure you talk about the Scripture reading and the "Later this Week" from the last time you got together.

Setup [1 minute]

When we worship idols, we offend God. Repentance and faith are the right responses when the Holy Spirit convicts us of idolatry.

Discover

Read [10 minutes]

When tempted, no one should say, "God is tempting me." For God cannot be tempted by evil, nor does he tempt anyone; but each person is tempted when they are dragged away by their own evil desire and enticed. Then, after desire has conceived, it gives birth to sin; and sin, when it is full-grown, gives birth to death. —James 1:13–15 (NIV)

For we do not have a high priest who is unable to empathize with our weak-

nesses, but we have one who has been tempted in every way, just as we are—yet he did not sin. —Hebrews 4:15 (NIV)

What does this passage say is the real source of temptation? Why Is it not wrong to be tempted?

What should we do when we are tempted?

Article: God is the Most Offended Party [10 minutes]

Consider again the idea that every sin is a finger-wagging accusation against God. This false worship is occurring at the heart level, where we are either believing lies about God or desiring something other than God. "With the heart a person believes" (Romans 10:10 NASB).

This heart-level perspective is a radical view of sin and repentance. It helps make sense of what David said in Psalm 51:4 (ESV) after he committed the sins of adultery and murder: "Against you, you only, have I sinned and done what is evil in your sight."

David stole another man's wife and then had that man killed. But he says he sinned against God? How can that be? David believed things in his heart that were not true about God, and believing those lies is what led him to commit adultery and murder. So it is as if David was looking at God and saying, "I believe I am more important than you. Therefore, I can lust after whatever my heart desires, regardless of what you have to say about it."

Can you see how this is a sin against God?

Unless we see God as the most offended party, we will not hate our sin.

When we repent, we cannot simply repent of our sinful actions, we must repent of our distorted worship!

This heart-level perspective is also a very helpful view of sin and transformation because it very clearly shows us the way out! Most of us think the way to stop sinning is to change our behavior. However if behind every sin is a lie about God, then what really needs to change is what I am believing in my heart! What really needs to change is my worship!

By now we probably all realize that we need to be transformed. We want to be the image of God the way we were intended to be His image, but transformation won't come by trying harder or gritting your teeth or clenching your fists. We call that "white-knuckling it." Many books and recovery programs are about behavior modification, but Jesus is about heart transformation. Jesus is about rightly directed worship.

Whatever sin pattern you find yourself struggling with right now, here's the reality: You worshipped your way into this situation, and by God's grace, you'll worship your way out.

Repentance and Faith

There are two major outcomes we hope to see through *Growing in Christ Together*:

1. We want to see how the sinful behaviors in our lives are really a result of distorted worship. We want to see how all of our sin is really a sin against a holy God, how God is the most offended party. This is the only thing that will lead to true repentance, which is the first step in transformation.
2. We want to learn how to express true faith in God. We want to know what right worship sounds like, both as a means of restoring fellowship with the Father and as a way of gaining victory in the moment of temptation.

Repentance means to change your mind. Specifically we're talking about changing what we believe about God. We've believed a lie—we must repent and exercise faith in the truth.

So what does repentance sound like? Since God is the most offended party, we must address Him with our repentance. We have looked at the Creator of the universe in the eye and made accusations against Him that are not true. We have set ourselves up as god. Because of this, we must acknowledge the grievous nature of our offense. Since we have believed lies about Him and desired things more than Him, we must go to the root of our rebellion. Repentance can not merely skim the surface of behavior ("God, I'm sorry I lied!"); true repentance plumbs the depths of the heart to discern the false worship that drove the behavior ("God, I repent of believing that your acceptance is not enough, and for lying to try and impress that girl. I desired her more than you.").

In the moment of temptation when you are tempted to worship something else than God, the right response is also worship. Don't just say to yourself, "God is good." Say it to Him. "Father, you are good. You are much better than what I was tempted to worship instead of you."

Without faith it is impossible to please God, because anyone who comes to him must believe that he exists and that he rewards those who earnestly seek him. —Hebrews 11:6 (NIV)

Faith in the character and nature of God is worship. If worship is ascribing worth to something, delighting in something, then exercising faith in God's character certainly qualifies.

Whether we've already sinned or we're being tempted to sin, faith sounds the same. It is an upward, God-directed affirmation of what we believe to be true about Him in the moment. So for the guy who lied to impress the girl, faith would sound like this: "God, you are the most glorious one! Your opinion of me is the only opinion that matters! You are good! You are enough! You satisfy every longing of my soul. In faith I affirm these things to be true of you."

Martin Luther is famous for saying that "all of life is repentance." May God give us the grace to walk out repentance and faith as often as needed, every single day.

Nurture [20 minutes]

Explain this sentence in your own words: "Unless we see God as the most offended party, we will not hate our sin."

Think about the sin you are addressing through your gospel change project. How is that sin an offense against God?

What are you saying to God when you are sinning? Do you believe He is the most offended party? What would right worship sound like in the moment of temptation?

Act [15 minutes]

Pray together concerning your gospel change project. Think about the truth you need to turn to in order to overcome that sin. What does true repentance sound like? What does right worship sound like? Begin writing this out.

Later This Week [1 minute]

Continue writing out your answers to the questions in the exercise. Spend extra time with God this week, repenting of your sin/idolatry and worshipping Him for who he truly is. This practice will be an invaluable tool in your fight against sin.

Put in place whatever reminders you need to do this. How might you be able to hold each other accountable?

Wrap it Up [5 minutes]

Briefly review what you learned today. Jot down the big-picture ideas in your own words. Discuss any final questions. Pray together.

This Week's Scripture Reading

We continue the narrative of Jesus in the Gospel of Luke. As you read these stories and teachings of Jesus, look for the truths about God that change who you are and how you live—specifically with repentance and faith. Who do we see Jesus to be in these stories, and what has He done through them? How does Jesus change who people are? What is He calling them to do? Lastly, we've discussed the gospel in many ways through this guide. On day five and six this week, you will read the historical account of Jesus' death and resurrection. How does this event change everything?

- Day 1: Luke 18:18–30
- Day 2: Luke 19:1–9
- Day 3: Luke 20:19–26
- Day 4: Luke 22: 7–30
- Day 5: Luke 23:18–56
- Day 6: Luke 24:1–12

Notes:

WEEK 14

Gospel Formation

Week 14

Big Picture

- Avoid the desires of the sinful nature/not sowing to the sinful nature
- Follow the desires of the Spirit/sowing to the Spirit
- Doing works in keeping with repentance

Opening [10 minutes]

Take a few minutes to see how each of you is doing and encourage each other. Be careful, as this time can easily get away from you. Make sure you talk about the Scripture reading and the "later this week" from the last time you got together.

Setup [1 minute]

By now you may have identified lies behind your sinful behavior and the truth you need to turn to in faith. You may have identified the idolatrous desires you need to turn from in repentance. Sadly, however, although understanding can be a big step forward, it does not equal change. Even if you have not fully analyzed your heart—and there may be issues behind issues—you still know the gospel truths and the gospel disciplines that will set you free. But the gospel disciplines of faith and repentance are a daily struggle. So, what strategies do you need to put in place to reinforce faith and repentance?[29]

Discover

Read [5 minutes]

Do not be deceived: God cannot be mocked. A man reaps what he sows. The one who sows to please his sinful nature, from that nature will reap destruction; the one who sows to please the Spirit, from the Spirit will reap eternal life.

—Galatians 6:7–8 (NIV)

So I say, live by the Spirit, and you will not gratify the desires of the sinful nature. For the sinful nature desires what is contrary to the Spirit, and the Spirit what is contrary to the sinful nature. —Galatians 5:16–17 (NIV)

› What does the saying "a man reaps what he sows" mean?
› What are the implications of this for our spiritual lives?
› Which desires are stronger in you: the desires of the sinful nature or the desires of the Spirit?

Article: What Strategies Do You Need to Reinforce Repentance and Faith? [10 minutes]

Our old nature has sinful desires—the idolatrous desires that cause sinful behavior and emotions. The Spirit has placed in the heart of every Christian a new desire: the desire for holiness. So we sow to the flesh whenever we do something that strengthens or provokes our sinful desires. We sow to the Spirit whenever we do something that strengthens our Spirit-inspired desire for holiness.[30]

It is not a mystical or complicated principle. Not sowing to the sinful nature means avoiding anything that might strengthen or provoke our sinful desires. It means saying no to the first stirrings of sinful desire in our hearts (mortification). It means avoiding situations where our sinful desires will be provoked. Sowing to the Spirit means doing whatever strengthens our Spirit-inspired desire for holiness. It means replacing the lies behind sin with the truth about God—His greatness and goodness.[31]

Avoiding the Desires of the Sinful Nature

No temptation has overtaken you but except what is common to man; and God is faithful, who will not allow you to be tempted beyond what you are able, but with the temptation will provide the way of escape also, so that you will be able to endure it. Therefore, my beloved, flee from idolatry.

—1 Corinthians 10:13–14 (NASB)

It is not a sin to be tempted. Jesus was tempted in every way, yet he was without sin (Hebrews 4:15). However, scripture is clear we are to take the way of escape that God gives from temptation ("flee!"). Jesus taught his followers to pray, "Lead us not into temptation."

We need to avoid situations in which we know we might particularly face temptation. We cannot change ourselves simply by avoiding temptation; change must begin within our hearts. However avoiding temptation does have a part to play. It is never the whole solution, but it can be part of the solution. As my friend Samuel puts it, "Avoidance buys us time." Sometimes sinful desires feel strong, but if there is no stimulation for those desires, there is time for the truth to prevail in my heart.[32]

Most of our sinful desires can be fed by things in our culture. The lies behind our sins are lies that are perpetuated at a community level. The world around us celebrates sinful desires and spreads lies about God. We cannot live in isolation from the world, but we can and should take steps to reduce its influence on us.[33]

John Stott sums up this whole idea well:

Every time we allow our mind to harbor a grudge, nurse a grievance, entertain an impure fantasy, or wallow in self-pity, we are sowing to the flesh. Every time we linger in bad company whose insidious influence we know we cannot resist, every time we lie in bed when we ought to be up and praying, every time we read pornographic literature, every time we take a risk which strains our self-control, we are sowing, sowing, sowing to the flesh. Some Christians sow to the flesh every day and wonder why they do not reap holiness.[34]

Following the Desires of the Spirit

The best way to keep down our sinful desires is to sow to the Spirit.[35] When

Paul tells Timothy to flee sinful desire, he always tells him to pursue righteousness in its place.

Flee the evil desires of youth, and pursue righteousness, faith, love and peace, along with those who call on the Lord out of a pure heart. —2 Timothy 2:22 (NIV)

Sowing to the Spirit means saying yes to whatever strengthens our Spirit-inspired desires. As we have seen, we sin when we believe lies about God. Sowing to the Spirit means filling our hearts with the truth about God. We sin because sinful desires matter more to us than God. We sow to the Spirit when we cultivate our love for God.

Here are five things that reinforce faith. Sometimes people call these "spiritual disciplines," but this is not helpful terminology. It can make Christian growth seem like an achievement on our part. In reality it is God who changes us through His grace. The only true spiritual disciplines in the Christian life are faith and repentance— actions that direct our attention to God's gracious activity. Instead it is better to use the traditional term: "the means of grace." These are ways God is gracious to us and by which He strengthens His work of grace in our hearts. They are the means God uses to feed our faith in Him. This is what sowing to the Spirit looks like in practice.[36]

1. Listening to the Scriptures

When Jesus prayed for His followers, he prayed, "Sanctify them by the truth; your word is truth." God has graciously revealed Himself to us through His Word, and He uses it to help transform us. Primarily, scripture does this by reminding us of the gospel—who God is, what He's done for us, who we are in light of that, and how we should live as a result. The Bible shows us the glory of Jesus over and over, revealing both our deep need for Him and His gracious provision of redemption for us. The Bible is the single most important resource for sowing to the Spirit.

2. Listening to God in Prayer

Our hunger for prayer should spring from two things: a desire to be with God Himself, and a deep awareness of our need for Him. Talking to the Father about Him and about our need for Him will transform us. By His grace, He has given us full access to Himself through Jesus. Why would we not go? J. C. Ryle says:

> *Praying and sinning will never live together in the same heart. Prayer will consume sin, or sin will choke prayer. . . . Diligence in prayer is the secret of eminent holiness. Without controversy there is a vast difference among true Christians. . . . I believe the difference in nineteen cases out of twenty arises from different habits about private prayer. I believe that those who are not eminently holy pray little, and those who are eminently holy pray much.*[37]

3. Corporate Worship

The root cause of sinful behavior and negative emotions is idolatrous desires. When we worship God we are reminding ourselves that God is bigger and better than anything sin offers.

One special means of grace is communion or the Lord's Supper. The bread and wine remind us we are now children of God through the death of Christ. They remind us that we belong to God because we were bought with the price of Christ's blood. They remind us that we do not need to prove ourselves because we are justified by Christ's blood. [39]

4. Community

One of the reasons God has put us in Christian communities is to help us change. We can't sow to the Spirit alone very effectively. The church is to be a community of change. We will think more about this next week. But here are some ways that the church is a means of grace:

› We remind one another of the truth.

- We are taught the Bible by people God has given for this purpose.
- We pray together for God's help.
- We model Christian change and holiness for one another.
- We see God at work in the lives of other people.
- We remind one another of God's greatness and goodness as we worship Him together.
- We are given opportunities for service.[38]

5. Mission

We often think of service as the fruit or sign of change, but it is also a means of grace that God uses to change us. Sin is fundamentally an orientation toward self. Serving God and others can help redirect us outward, taking our attention away from ourselves. Serving others in practical ways is a great prescription for people suffering from negative emotions. When we are self-absorbed, we focus on our problems and successes. Serving others is a great way of turning from a preoccupation with yourself. [40]

Nurture [15 minutes]

What are some ways you sow to the flesh?

What temptations do you need to avoid? How will you do that?

How are you being proactive to sow to the Spirit?

Which gospel formation "activity" above do you avoid, lack, or need to grow in? Why?

How does the gospel give us power to walk in repentance?

Pray Together [20 minutes]

At this point, you know each other well. Spend time laboring in prayer for each other. Spend about seven minutes focusing on each person with the others praying for his or her life in Christ, gospel understanding, and repentance and joy in the gospel.

Act [10 minutes]

Which of the means of grace would you like to practice more regularly? Why?

How can we encourage each other this week to pursue formation in the gospel?

Later This Week [3 minutes]

You're heading into the final few weeks of this study. Make plans for the final week to make the completion of this guide a special moment and a marker in your discipleship journey.

Wrap it Up [5 minutes]

Briefly review what you learned today. Jot down the big-picture ideas in your own words. Discuss any final questions. Pray together.

This Week's Scripture Reading:

This week we'll read key stories from the book of Acts. As you read these stories look for the truths about God that change who you are and how you live. Who is God as He forms the Church? What is the Spirit like? What has the Spirit done? How does the Spirit change who people are? What does the Spirit call and empower people to do?

- Day 1: Acts 1:4–9
- Day 2: Acts 2:14–21
- Day 3: Acts 2:22–36
- Day 4: Acts 2:37–47
- Day 5: Acts 11:19–30 & Acts 13:1–3
- Day 6: Acts 16:1–1

Notes:

WEEK 15

Community

Week 15

Big Picture

- The role of community in shaping, sending, and discipling us
- Our role in community to disciple others
- Repentance and faith expressed through participation in the mission of God.

Opening [10 minutes]

Take a few minutes to see how each of you is doing and encourage each other. Be careful, as this time can easily get away from you. Make sure you talk about the "Later this week" from the last time you got together.

Setup [2 minutes]

We've spent the bulk of the last fourteen weeks talking about who we are as individuals. However, we don't sin, believe, or grow up in our faith in vacuum. Furthermore, real change happens in the context of community.

How would you describe your experiences with "Christian community"?

Leader's Note

This week doesn't have a specific passage to read because the article dives into several. Don't hesitate pausing or discussing the passages with the "Four Questions" after you read the article.

Discover

Article: Stepping into Community [15 Minutes]

The dominant metaphor for Christian community throughout the New Testament is family. God is Father: We are adopted by Him through Christ, we are brothers and sisters, we are heirs, and we have received every spiritual blessing. From Abraham onward, God's purposes of blessing and salvation are worked out through a family. From Jesus' death and resurrection onward, the Church becomes a diverse family belonging to a community and belonging to God. The family of God is characterized by the Father, who is loving, compassionate, gracious, merciful, patient, and just. Those who have been adopted into salvation are no longer orphans because of sin, but belong because of God's love.

It is from this place of experience and knowledge of divine love that anyone is able to love others within community. We receive grace so we can extend grace to our brothers in Christ. It is from knowing God's patience and mercy that we live patiently and mercifully with our family. Christian community is authentic, generous, and caring because God is truth, grace, and love.

This sort of family is not an ideal we have to realize, but rather it is a reality created by God in Christ in which we participate. Instead of finding our motivation in our own prescribed needs and desires, we cling to loving one other because we have received God's love. Christian community is one of consistent and mutual extension of grace, truth, faith, hope, and love not for the sake of receiving it but from the joy of giving.

Growing in Love by Giving Yourself

Within this familial community, each of the "one another commands" makes sense:

- Comfort one another (2 Cor. 13:11)

- Agree with one another (2 Cor. 13:11)
- Live in peace with one another (2 Cor. 13:11)
- Greet one another (2 Cor. 13:11)
- Bear one another's burdens—which in context refers to confronting sin and being burdened for the sinful brother (Gal. 6:2)
- Bear with one another (Eph. 4:2)
- Encourage one another (1 Thess. 5:11)
- Build one another up (1 Thess. 5:11)
- Do not grumble against one another (James 5:9)
- Do not speak evil against one another (James 4:11)

Through these "one-another's" we become family in experience. These commands are the process and action toward an authentic life of community where people care for one another. They are also commands that say unequivocally that community is a place of giving of yourself.

Being a member of God's family requires death to self. You must die. Community is costly. As the Apostle Paul write in Colossians 3:9, put off the old self:

Do not lie to one another, seeing that you have put off the old self with its practices and have put on the new self, which is being renewed in knowledge after the image of its creator. Here there is not Greek and Jew, circumcised and uncircumcised, barbarian, Scythian, slave, free; but Christ is all, and in all.
—Colossians 3:9–11 (ESV)

Here Paul is telling us exactly the way toward familial community: Become new through God and be formed in the image of God. All of this sounds very utopian and pleasant. Who wouldn't want to be "fixed" and experience a caring and authentic community where your burdens are carried, you are not alone, and you are known? We all would, but a community like this is costly. It requires a death to you. It requires leaving your identity in yourself—what you do, what you have, where you came from.

In the place of this dying self, you will cling to the new self, which is being formed by God and is in the image of God. The way toward an authentic community is God recreating us. In Christ, we are not known by our culture, ethnicity, status, or resources. Those labels do not fit within a missional community because we are all defined by Christ. He is recreating every aspect of our hearts.

Paul then goes on to describe the cost and fruit of this new identity in Christ:

Put on then, as God's chosen ones, holy and beloved, compassionate hearts, kindness, humility, meekness, and patience, bearing with one another and, if one has a complaint against another, forgiving each other; as the Lord has forgiven you, so you also must forgive. And above all these put on love, which binds everything together in perfect harmony. And let the peace of Christ rule in your hearts, to which indeed you were called in one body. And be thankful. Let the word of Christ dwell in you richly, teaching and admonishing one another in all wisdom, singing psalms and hymns and spiritual songs, with thankfulness in your hearts to God. And whatever you do, in word or deed, do everything in the name of the Lord Jesus, giving thanks to God the Father through him. —Colossians 3:12–17 (ESV)

We exchange our self-interested, self-defined, and approval-seeking lives for one where we know we are approved of and chosen by God. The new life is one in community where we live with pure and loved hearts. Now we clothe our lives with kindness and humility! This is how we bear with one another, how we forgive one another: by being made new by God, by receiving new hearts of compassion.

Paul then points to key pillar of community: forgiveness. You will not hold grudges, judge others, snicker behind others' backs, figure our what their problem is and hold it over them, or force them to earn your acceptance through right living. No, you don't get to do any of those things, and you don't want to. Instead you forgive.

How can you forgive? You have been forgiven. In other words, you received compassion from God who did not snicker at you or make you earn His approval. With a firsthand knowledge of being accepted, welcomed, and forgiven, you extend it to others. This will stretch you.

The pattern of life in this world is to use others' mistakes, errors, and missteps against them and for you. Our sins define us, and their sins define them. However, in Christ we are defined by the love God poured out on us to forgive us our sins. We are defined by that love. This love rules in community. This love overcomes burdens. This truth brings peace amidst all kinds of suffering. This grace produces thankful hearts. This is the love of Jesus. Paul says this love rules community (1 Cor. 13).

You could sum up all of the one-another commands in the New Testament into this one: Love one another. What kind of love? The greatest kind of love: self-donating and self-giving love. The love exemplified by Jesus on the cross, where He gave His life: body, presence, and future. On the cross we see the love that is required within His community. We see on the cross the commandment lived out. Jesus doesn't ask us to live out an ideal for our sake or require us to do something He will not do. Jesus is calling us to be conformed into the image of the Creator. To be like Jesus is to love like He loved and to extend that love to the ones He chose to love. This is why we love one another. What are the implications of letting this love rule our hearts as we live alongside others?

- We don't give from the margins.
- We don't give from convenience.
- We don't give from comfort.
- We don't give our leftovers.
- We don't give from insecurity.

Rather we . . .

- We give ourselves with joy.
- We give ourselves with generosity.
- We give ourselves with truth.
- We give ourselves with humility.
- We give ourselves with forgiveness.
- We give ourselves with confidence, not allowing our community to live in sin, worship idols, and disregard Jesus as savior.
- We give because God gave Christ.
- We love because Christ loved us.

This is the type of familial community our souls actually crave. This is the only expectation big enough for lasting community.

The Ideal: Growing in Devotion and Unity

This is what happens in the book of Acts after the people had heard the gospel preached by Peter and responded to it in repentance and belief. After they received the gospel they changed the way they lived together:

"And they devoted themselves to the apostles' teaching and the fellowship, to the breaking of bread and the prayers. And awe came upon every soul, and many wonders and signs were being done through the apostles. And all who believed were together and had all things in common. And they were selling their possessions and belongings and distributing the proceeds to all, as any had need. And day by day, attending the temple together and breaking bread in their homes, they received their food with glad and generous hearts, praising God and having favor with all the people. And the Lord added to their number day by day those who were being saved." —Acts 2:42–47 (ESV)

The two key words in this passage are "devotion" and "together." Devotion means to persist with closely or serve personally. In other words, attach yourself to the service of another. Here we see a glimpse of the early church, a community of people who were devoted not only to Jesus but also to one another. We see a beautiful picture of the results of a community of people who were so devoted to the gospel that they were devoted to one another. There isn't even a taste of self-focused consuming of relationships or the desperate seeking of fulfillment from others. Instead, they were a people secure in God's grace and salvation who engaged community as people full and ready to give.

Connected to this devotion is their togetherness or their finding all things in common—unity. Their devotion to Jesus and one another resulted in unity. They lived more like a tight family than a loose collection of individuals. They didn't consume each other. They clung to the gospel. You don't get unity by being nice, tolerant, or experts in conflict resolution strategies. Paul describes the cause of our unity in Ephesians 4:1–6 *(ESV)*:

I therefore, a prisoner for the Lord, urge you to walk in a manner worthy of the calling to which you have been called, with all humility and gentleness, with patience, bearing with one another in love, eager to maintain the unity of the Spirit in the bond of peace. There is one body and one Spirit—just as you were called to the one hope that belongs to your call— one Lord, one faith, one baptism, one God and Father of all, who is over all and through all and in all.

Paul connects his charge for their unity, love, caring, and patience to their common Lord. Paul says, you are one (unified) because you have one Lord, one faith, one baptism, and one God. You achieve unity not through rules of engagement but through a shared ruler over all life. We live as family because we all belong to "one God and Father." This is why we are eager to maintain unity.

The church in Acts 2 expresses their devotion and unity in activity. Community is not simply an idea we think about but requires action and obedience. This community prayed together, and they ate together. They shared the gospel teachings, and they shared their possessions to meet needs! They welcomed others into their homes, and they received from one another with generous hearts. They did not live in a holy huddle or commune, but they did share moments of life in meals and in their homes. More importantly, they shared the struggles of life and the joys of life. Therefore the ideal community is one growing in devotion and unity. This is the biblical pattern.

Nurture [25 minutes]

What would it take to recover this biblical pattern of community?

What keeps us from being part of a group committed to being a community of people devoted to Jesus and one another?

How do the idolatry, sins, and false gospels we've discussed in previous weeks impact how we relate in community?

How does the truth of the gospel free us to participate in this kind of biblical community?

Act [15 minutes]

Discuss ways your Christian community embodies the characteristics described in the Scriptures. How does it fall short? What is God leading you to do and be within those communities? How is God leading you to engage church as family?

Later This Week [5 minutes]

We can step into this type of community through serving one another, blessing one another, and spending time together. Spend a few minutes thinking about the people in this DNA group or in your missional community. Who can you serve, bless, or spend time with next week?

Wrap it Up [2 minutes]

Briefly review what you learned today. Jot down the big-picture ideas in your own words. Discuss any final questions. Pray together.

This Week's Scripture Reading:

For our final week of Scripture reading, we are going to return to the book of Ephesians. This time, we will read an entire chapter each day. As you read consider underlining or highlighting one key phrase or truth from each paragraph you need to believe as you engage a life of discipleship.

- Day 1: Ephesians 1 S
- Day 2: Ephesians 2 M
- Day 3: Ephesians 3 T
- Day 4: Ephesians 4 W
- Day 5: Ephesians 5 T
- Day 6: Ephesians 6 F

Notes:

WEEK 16

Mission

Week 16

Big Picture

- The role of mission in shaping, shepherding, and discipling us
- Our role in community to disciple others
- Repentance and faith expressed through participation in the mission of God

Opening [10 minutes]

Take a few minutes to see how each of you is doing and encourage each other. Be careful, as this time can easily get away from you. Make sure you talk about the "later this week" from the last time you got together.

Setup [10 minutes]

How would you describe your calling to participate in God's mission?

How does the transformation you've experienced shape how you share the gospel?

Discover

Read [15 Minutes]

Now the eleven disciples went to Galilee, to the mountain to which Jesus had directed them. And when they saw him they worshiped him, but some doubted. And Jesus came and said to them, "All authority in heaven and on earth has been given to me. Go therefore and make disciples of all nations, baptizing them in the name of the Father and of the Son and of the Holy Spirit, teaching them to observe all that I have commanded you. And behold, I am with you always, to the end of the age." —Matthew 28:16–20 (ESV)

What does Jesus claim about Himself? What are the implications of Jesus having all authority on your life?

What is the good news in this passage?

If everything we've read is true and Jesus is LORD, what weight does this commission have on our lives?

What would faithfulness to this passage look like?

Article: The Gospel Isn't a Cul-De-Sac [15 Minutes]

The cul-de-sac was a phenomenal invention for the suburbs. It created a safe and peaceful place for families to raise children.

No one passed through. In fact, the only time strangers can appear is after a wrong turn and they find themselves at the dead end. The design made it simple for those who don't belong to quickly turn around.

It also kept everyone who belonged there in one place. Once you came in, you didn't have to leave. You could remain the rest of your days with likeminded folks, playing games in your asphalt sanctuary.

The cul-de-sac is the epitome of the suburban life and values. However, the gospel is not a cul-de-sac. It isn't a safe sanctuary that separates you from the dangers of the world—it throws you into the world. It isn't your private enclave to secure your values and doctrines. It ushers you into a hospitality for the other—the not-like-you. The gospel is doctrinal, changing what we believe. It also is personal, changing who we are, but it is more than that.

The Gospel is Missional: It Changes Where & How We Live. [1]

If we just focus on the doctrinal and personal aspect of the gospel, we will neglect its missional aspect. If the doctrinal gospel changes what we believe and the personal gospel changes who we are, then the missional gospel changes where we live and what we say. It is the hopeful announcement that God is making all things new in Christ Jesus! The gospel ushers us into a new kingdom and new world. We no longer live in a world dominated by death and deconstruction but one of life and re-creation!

The Spirit of the Lord is upon me, because he has anointed me to proclaim good news to the poor. He has sent me to proclaim liberty to the captives and recovering of sight to the blind, to set at liberty those who are oppressed, to proclaim the year of the Lord's favor. —Luke 4:18–19, Isaiah 61 (ESV)

The Gospel Changes Everything

The gospel changes everything. It is not only good news for us, but also for our neighbors, the poor, our city, and the world. It affects the social, cultural, and physical fabric of the universe. In Luke 4, Jesus preached the gospel to the poor, marginalized, and oppressed. It is good news for them because through His death and resurrection He has defeated sin, death, and evil (1 Jn. 2:13; 3:8). The gospel announces the in-breaking reign of Jesus, which is in the process of reversing the order of things. The poor become rich, the captives are freed, and the old become new.

The Gospel Sends Us on Mission

Those who follow Jesus join His mission by making disciples of all ethnic groups by going, teaching, and baptizing (Matt. 28:18–20). We are sent to teach, speak, counsel, discuss, and proclaim the gospel to others so they might be baptized into God's new creation and join His mission of making all things new. We are called ambassadors of reconciliation and given the privilege of sharing in Jesus's ministry of reconciling the world to Himself (2 Cor. 5:17–20). Those who have been changed by the gospel share its life-changing power with others. We should announce and embody the good news by caring for the poor and rebuilding cities (Is. 61:4). In fact, the future for the people of God is an entirely new city in a new creation (Rev. 21). The church should be a movie trailer of this grand, coming attraction when all things will be made new!

Remember This is Who You Are

The result of the Church—you, us—being sent is that we live as a community of disciples, not only devoted to Jesus and to one another, but devoted to our neighbors and our city, too. When we come to Christ, we are all sent on His mission.

We are new and have a new purpose. Christ reconciled us to Himself, and we are a new creation. Our old way of finding identity and our broken ways of finding meaning are over. We are reconciled and ushered into a vibrant and living relationship with God. This is the gospel, that Christ has reconciled us to God through His death and resurrection and is making all things new—even us. We are recipients of the gospel, messengers of the gospel, servants of the gospel, and representatives of the gospel's work. See, you cannot separate our identity in Christ from our purpose in Christ. That identity and purpose requires some sort of expression of gospel-focused community on mission:

- We live on mission because we have received the gospel.
- We live on mission because we are messengers of the gospel. He is making His appeal to the world through us.
- We live on mission because we are ministers of reconciliation—servants of the gospel.
- We live on mission because we are ambassadors—representatives of the gospel.

Nurture [20 minutes]

How have you tried to make the gospel a cul-de-sac?

How do your sin, idols, and unbelief impact the way you engage God's mission?

How can the work the Spirit is doing in you move through you to make disciples of others?

How has your understanding of the gospel through this guide impacted the way you engage your neighbors, co-workers, and friends? Why?

Act [10 minutes]

Who is God calling you to disciple?

How will you engage the mission of God as the purpose of your life?

Choose a Path Forward

Leader's Note

You might not have time for this discussion; however, you will want to make a plan for the group moving forward. You could make this your entire conversation the following week.

Should we continue? Are we still committed to each other and this process?

Should we multiply this group? Are there members of this group who could lead and start another group?

Is there anyone we should add to this DNA group? Are there people in our community we should bring in?

What should we use to guide us? At this point, you've grown in discover, nurture, and act (DNA). Consider selecting a book from the Bible to walk through those three steps on your own, or consider using another guide. Here are a few good compliments to this:

- *The Gospel Fluency Handbook*: designed to help you and your group become fluent in the gospel—in other words, to help you move from unbelief to belief. Available at *saturatetheworld.com*

- *4 G's*: explore in more depth the truths summarized in week eleven. Available at *saturatetheworld.com*
- *The True Story*: explore the six movements of the Story of God in this six-week guide. Available at *saturatetheworld.com*

Wrap it Up [10 minutes]

You just finished sixteen intensive weeks examining sin, Scripture, and the gospel in deep community. Spend time writing down the big-picture truths and growth from this journey. As you look back, share these big things with each other and pray for each other.

Notes:

Epilogue

The process of becoming more like Jesus will not end until we see Him face-to-face. Here are some parting thoughts as you move forward in your journey as a disciple.

Gospel Transformation

We began with Paul's words that the gospel "is the power of God that brings salvation to everyone who believes" (Romans 1:16 NIV). Stay rooted in the fact that you are not what you do—you are what's been done for you by Jesus.

Continue to walk in the habit of repentance and faith! Use your deepened understanding of the gospel to root out sin in your life. Keep asking, "What does repentance sound like?" and "What does right worship sound like?" Turn from sin and worship God from the heart over and over again.

Change Happens in Community

We desperately need each other. Speak the truth in love to one another in community. Remind each other of your gospel identity. Let the gospel shape all of your relationships and all of your interactions. Submit the big decisions of your life to a community centered around the gospel.

The Mission: Make Disciples Who Make Disciples

There are only a few things we can do on earth we can't do in heaven—sin and make disciples. Jesus has left us here to make disciples. Don't delay in beginning a new DNA relationship. Pursue gospel change with a friend, a neighbor, or someone from your missional community. Imagine the thrill of leading others to the point of being able to lead someone else toward greater dependence on the Spirit of Christ! There's nothing else like it on earth.

Appendix 1

The Structure of DNA Groups

How Many Should Be in a DNA Group?

Discipleship methods have often employed a one-on-one approach. While this is certainly in line with many apprenticeship models (from which we can glean a lot about how to train someone along the way), it does not appear to be the method Jesus utilized. We rarely, if ever, find Him with only one of His disciples. In our experience as a church family, we have found that three is the ideal size for a DNA group.

If you are accustomed to one-on-one meetings, there's a number of reasons to add a third person:

- A more-dynamic group exchange occurs.
- It is much more difficult for one person to dominate the conversation.
- There are two sets of ears filtering everything that is said, providing two unique perspectives in response.
- There's a much greater potential for learning and development. Each person is unique and brings so much to the table.
- Here are two people loving and supporting each person in the group. No one is bearing another's burdens alone.

On the other hand, if you are accustomed to small groups of four to eight, there's a number of reasons to limit it to three:

- Each person can contribute significantly to the group.
- No one can "hide," remaining silent for very long before someone asks, "What do you think?"
- Each person has an ample opportunity to share at each group meeting.
- Scheduled group meetings don't last multiple hours.

Though three is the ideal size, circumstances will sometimes dictate that a group be larger than three. Schedule conflicts and a lack of qualified leaders can lead to groups of four, five, and even six meeting together for a time. While not ideal, these options are better than only two people meeting on a consistent basis.

Appendix 2

TELLING YOUR STORY WITH JESUS AS THE HERO

Putting Together Your Gospel Story

Understanding God's Story is essential for properly interpreting the creation-fall-redemption-restoration elements in our own story. Though we regularly believe that our stories are about us, our stories are really about God. "In him we live and move and have our being" (Acts 17:28 NIV).

Your story is ultimately God's Story. It's by Him and about Him. Your story is good news, a story about God's redemption of a broken person. He is the main character and the hero, not you. "For from him and through him and to him are all things. To him be the glory forever" (Romans 11:36 CSB).

Think through the four elements of your story, and consider how each one is an opportunity to point to your need for God and His work. Our stories consist of a countless string of smaller scenes, so begin by praying and asking the Holy Spirit to show you which parts you should include in your gospel story.

Creation

We all have a fundamental belief about our origin—who or what gave us our existence, made us who we are, and shaped us into the person we are today. God's Story begins with Him bringing everything into existence. He is the author and main character of the Story, and all things find their worth and value in Him.

All of us have looked to someone or something other than God to define us, to give us a sense of worth and value. As you begin your gospel story, talk about your background, some early shaping influences, and what gave you your sense of worth and value.

Key Themes: Origin, Identity

Key Gospel Question: Who or what most shaped your understanding of yourself? What were the sources of your sense of personal value and identity?

Other questions to consider:

- Where were you born, and what was going on in your family at the time?
- Talk about your relationships with your family members (parents, siblings, or other important people).
- Early on, who and what were some of the main influences in your life?
- What did you believe about God?

Fall

The world we live in is not as it should be. We are not as we should be. Brokenness is all around us. We have deeply held convictions about why things are broken. We often tend to place the blame at the feet of others: parents, siblings, friends, teachers, leaders, and even the government.

God's Story shows us that our own sin is the primary thing that wreaks havoc on our lives. As you tell your gospel story, talk about specific ways your sin brought about pain and destruction in your life. Include failed attempts at fixing the brokenness in your life.

Key Themes: Brokenness, Blame

Key Gospel Question: How was your relationship with God and others not the way God created it to be? Why?

Other questions to consider:

- What were some of your most painful experiences?
- How did you respond to the pain?
- What was broken in your life? Relationships? Behavior? Attitudes? Health?
- Who was to blame for this brokenness?
- How did you try to fix the brokenness? Were those efforts effective?

Redemption

All of us look to created things to save us, to rescue us, to give us signifcance, and to make us right. Money, possessions, acceptance, approval, relationships, and achievements all seem to offer some hope for repairing the brokenness in our lives. Education, government, recreation, and self-fulfillment can grab our attention as potential saviors, too, but the gospel tells a different story! The redemption movement of your story has the potential to be very powerful because you get to declare your faith in Jesus as the One who has saved and rescued you. Talk specifically about how you placed your trust in Jesus to save and rescue you from your sin and from the brokenness in your life. Describe how Jesus' life, death, and resurrection have brought redemption to specific broken parts of your story.

Key Themes: Rescue, Deliverance

Key Gospel Question: How has Jesus redeemed and rescued you through His death on the cross? How did you come to put your faith and trust in Him to save you and restore your life to the way God intended it to be?

Other questions to consider:

- What people or things failed to rescue you?
- How did the Spirit lead you to put your faith in Jesus? Did He use people, the Bible, a supernatural experience, difficult circumstances, or a powerful message?
- What were some of the effects of your belief in Jesus? How did you begin to experience God restoring you back to the way you were originally created?

Restoration

There's a deep longing within each of us for change, for things to be different tomorrow than they are today. For some, this means finding a job or a spouse. Others hope for world peace and a fair distribution of resources, a Utopian society. The desire to "have it all" is a longing that many share. What we're all craving is a mending of the brokenness that surrounds us. We want restoration, but we want it to look a certain way.

Because of what Jesus has done, restoration has begun. We are a new creation, and we've been made right with the Father! In God's Story, restoration means that His image-bearers begin to live in the way they were originally created to live. His Spirit lives in and through us, making us more like Jesus, even though we are still living in a fallen, broken world. Conclude your gospel story by talking about what the Spirit is doing in your life now. Share some evidences of His grace, indicators that you've been made new, that His restorative work has already begun in you.

Key Themes: Hope, Transformation

Key Gospel Question: What has changed and is changing in your life now? Who and what is the focus of your life today?

Other questions to consider:

› What are you hoping will change next week, month, year, ten years?

› Who is the focus of your preferred version of the future?

› What are some specific ways you've seen the Spirit make you more like Jesus (consider the fruit of the Spirit in Galatians 5:22–23)? Examine restoration in your attitude, your behavior, and your relationships, and be as specific as you can.

› What aspect of the new heavens and new earth are you most excited about?

A Few Story Tips

- Make your story about ten minutes long.
- It's not essential, but you may want to consider writing out your story. This will help you stay on track and will ensure you include the most important aspects.
- Use normal, everyday language to tell your story.
- The Father already knows your story and accepts you fully because of Jesus, so you can be totally honest with others. Don't fear what people might think.
- Practice telling your story with close friends and family so you will be prepared when needed.
- Be prepared to share your gospel story in the midst of spiritual conversations with not-yet believers. Anytime the conversation turns to God, Jesus, Church, or the Bible, it might be a great opportunity to share how Jesus is the hero of your story.
- Pray and ask the Spirit to speak through you as you tell your story.

Remember, It's Actually His Story!

Appendix 3

ENGAGING PERSONAL STORIES IN DNA GROUPS

Here are Some Things to Listen for in a Person's Story

Emotional words: "I'm angry." "I'm afraid." "I was really hurt."

Interpretive words: "This shouldn't happen." "I guess I'm getting what I deserve." "I wonder if it's even worth getting up in the morning."

Self-talk: "I am such a failure." "I am not smart enough, pretty enough, etc."

Listen closely for pride and insecurity: "I have accomplished this and this and this." "I always got good grades and performed well in various activities."

God-talk: "I tried hard to obey God." "How could God let this happen to me?"

Listen closely for denial, blame, and an unwillingness to take responsibility: "God's never done anything for me." "God is punishing me."

Stated motives: "I wanted to get even. I wanted revenge." "I was so ashamed, I decided to never tell my parents." "I need people to like me. I need their approval." "I feel so guilty, I could never forgive myself."

Patterns of behavior, positive or negative. Listen closely for power and control.

Destructive or repeated sin: "I started using drugs when I was twelve."

Listen closely for sources of comfort and self-medicating: "I smoked pot every day for five or six years." "I slept with more women than I can count."

Abuse or neglect: "My dad would scream at me if I came home with C's." "I was raped by my step-brother when I was twelve." "I used to play alone in my room most of the time." "The kids at school used to call me fat."

Listen for mom and dad: "I've never met my dad." "My mom gave me everything I wanted." "My dad said he wished I was never born." "I don't remember my dad hugging me." "Nothing was ever good enough for my mom."

Encouragement After Their Story

- Thank you for sharing your story. It is an honor to hear it!
- Your story is an amazing story about God and His work (most people will not see this, but you should say it anyway). God is in this!
- It is very easy to focus on your circumstances at a time like this. I completely understand. God is primarily concerned with your heart in this situation. He wants to keep pulling your focus up out of the mire of your circumstances and onto Him. Keep watching for your heart responses in the midst of this trial.

Specific Questions for Further Clarity (If Needed)

- Tell me about your relationship with your dad.
- How did you feel when that significant event happened?
- Did that hurtful situation ever get resolved?
- How old were you when that happened?

General Questions

- Where are you still struggling to believe the gospel?
- How has this situation helped you see your sin more clearly?
- Where do you see God at work in this situation?

References

[1] Tim Chester, You Can Change: God's Transforming Power for Our Sinful Behavior & Negative Emotions (Nottingham: Inter-Varsity Press, 2008), 42-43.

[2] Chester, You Can Change, 34.

[3] J.I. Packer, Knowing God. (Downers Grove, IL: Inter-Varsity, 1973/1993), 201-202

[4] Chester, You Can Change, 35-42.

[5] Chester, You Can Change, 46.

[6] Chester, You Can Change, 47-48.

[7] Adapted from John Piper, "How the Spirit Does What the Law Could Not Do", http://www.desiringgod.org/resource-library/sermons/how-the-spirit-does-what-the-law-could-not-do

[8] Tim Keller, "Redeemer Vision Paper #1: The Gospel: Key to Change". http://www.redeemer2.com/visioncampaign/papers/Vision_Paper_1-The_Gospel-The_Key_to_Change.pdf.

[9] Chester, You Can Change, 67.

[10] Chester, You Can Change, 76.

[11] Chester, You Can Change, 76.

[12] Chester, You Can Change, 77.

[13] Chester, You Can Change, 79.

[14] This analogy is from a sermon by Jonathan Edwards called 'A Divine and Supernatural Light,' Works Vol. 2 (Bell, Arnold & Co., 1840), 12-17.

Chester, You Can Change, 88.

[16] Edward T. Welch, When People are Big and God is Small (P&R, 1997).

[17] Edward T. Welch, When People are Big and God is Small (P&R, 1997), 15.

[18] Chester, You Can Change, 91-92.

[19] Chester, You Can Change, 104.

[20] Chester, You Can Change, 106.

[21] G.K. Beale, We Become What we Worship: A Biblical Theology of Idolatry (Downers Grove: Inter-Varsity, 2008), 203-204

[22] Timothy Keller, Counterfeit Gods: The Empty Promises of Money, Sex, and Power, and the Only Hope That Matters (New York: Dutton, 2009), xvii-xix.

[29] Chester, You Can Change, 145.

[30] Chester, You Can Change, 146.

[31] Summarized from Chester, You Can Change, 145-152.

[32] Chester, You Can Change, 147.

[33] Chester, You Can Change, 148.

[34] John Stott, The Message of Galatians (IVP, 1968), 170.

[35] Chester, You Can Change, 152.

[36] Chester, You Can Change, 153.

[37] J. C. Ryle, Practical Religion (Banner of Truth, 1878, 1998), 71, 74-75.

[38] Chester, You Can Change, 157.

[39] Chester, You Can Change, 157-158.

[40] Chester, You Can Change, 158-159.

[41] Thune and Walker, "Gospel Centered Life", 46-47.

[42] Adapted from Mike Wilkerson, Redemption (Seattle: Mars Hill Church, 2009), Appendix 2, 94-97.

About the Contributors

Justin Kuravackal:

Justin gets to serve Soma Federal Way as an elder and missional community leader alongside his wife, Kate (a partner in mission for over 20 years and in three countries: US, Venezuela, and Texas). They are blessed with two amazing kids. Justin had a hand in creating The Story-Formed Way and other resources. For fun, the whole fam is training as black belts in Taekwondo.

Abe Meysenburg:

Abe Meysenburg has served as a pastor/elder with Soma Tacoma since 2007, as well as serving on the board for the larger Soma Family of Churches (wearesoma.com). In addition to preaching regularly, he oversees all of the shepherding ministries of Soma Tacoma, and continually works to equip other leaders to shepherd and teach, as well. Abe and Jennifer are both graduates of Moody Bible Institute. They have four children - Abby, Julia, Luke, and Noah.

Jeff Vanderstelt:

Jeff is a pastor, speaker, author, and founder and visionary leader of Saturate and the Soma Family of Churches. He serves as a teaching pastor and Director of Missional Communities at Doxa Church in Bellevue, WA. Additionally, he serves on the Advisory Board of the C2C Network. He and Jayne, his wife of twenty-five years, have three children; Haylee, Caleb, and Maggie.

Brad Watson:

Brad A. Watson (M.A. in Theology) enjoys encouraging, challenging, and helping followers of Jesus to live on mission in community by helping them connect the gospel with its implications to their daily lives. Locally, Brad serves as an equipping elder of Soma Culver City in Los Angeles, California, where he lives with his wife and their three children. Globally, he has the privilege of coaching and resourcing church leaders on how to form gospel-centered communities that love God and serve their city.

Thanks for using *Growing in Christ Together.*

Here are a few other resources for immersing yourself in God's story and growing in your understanding of the gospel:

Subscribe to the Saturate Podcast

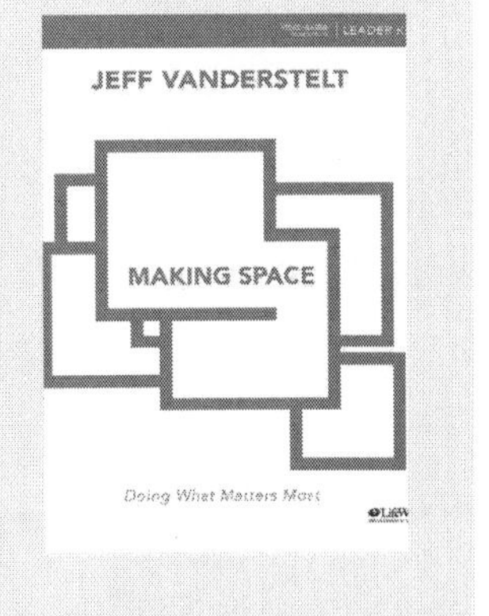

@SaturateWorld

/saturatetheworld

SaturateWorld

/saturatetheworld

Made in the USA
Middletown, DE
08 December 2022